ESL DRAMA START

Drama Activities for
ESL Learners

First published in 2017 by
JemBooks
Cork,
Ireland
www.dramastartbooks.com

ISBN: 978-0-9935506-1-4

Typesetting by Gough Typesetting Service, Dublin

ESL DRAMA START

DRAMA ACTIVITIES FOR ESL LEARNERS

Julie Meighan

JemBooks

About the Author

Julie Meighan is a lecturer in Drama in Education at the Cork Institute of Technology. She has taught Drama to all age groups and levels. She is the author of the Amazon bestselling *Drama Start: Drama Activities, Plays and Monologues for Young Children (Ages 3 -8)* ISBN 978-0956896605, *Drama Start Two: Drama Activities and Plays for Children (Ages 9-12)* ISBN 978-0-9568966-1-2 and *Stage Start: 20 Plays for Children (Ages 3-12)* ISBN 978-0956896629.

Contents

Co-Operative Activities

Concentration Activities

Imagination Activities

Movement Activities

Improvisation

Storytelling Activities

Puppet Activities

PART TWO: PLAYS

Introduction

ESL Drama Start consists of over one hundred drama games and plays that can be use in the English language classroom. Drama games are a perfect tool to use in any classroom that encompasses multiple learning styles, ability levels and age groups. In addition, the activities in this book help ESL students to access active language in an effective and imaginative way. The activities facilitate students' ability to learn in different ways as visual learners, auditory learners and kinaesthetic learners. Part one contains drama games that are divided into ten sections, which not only enables the young learners to improve self-confidence, build trust, communicate effectively and develop creativity, but they can also have a profound effect on literary development, academic success and social interaction. The games help students to explore creativity, communication, mime, movement, improvisation, puppets and storytelling while developing their listening and concentration skills. The drama games are fun, challenging and rewarding, not only for the students but also for the educators/ leaders themselves.

Part two of this book contains six simple plays that can be used as performance plays, readers' theatre or used to promote reading in groups. Each play is between five and ten minutes long. The plays can be adapted to suit the various needs of the group. The cast list is very flexible and more characters can be added. Characters can be changed or omitted. In addition, the teacher/group leader can assume the role of the storyteller if the students are unable to read or not at the reading level required.

Props/costume/stage directions:
There are a minimal number of props needed for these plays. Costumes can be very simple. The students can wear clothes that are the same colour as their animal. They can wear a mask or use some face paint. All suggestions for stage directions are included in brackets and italics.

Part One: Drama Games

Some Practical Advice for Teachers before You Begin

- *Introduce drama into your language class slowly. Students maybe lacking in confidence, especially if English is not their first language. Start with very simple warm-up games such as The Name Game or Greetings. Once you have built a sense of trust and teamwork, begin to focus on more complex and exploratory games or on games that demand a student's involvement.*
- *Choose the right activity for the class. You must know what you want to achieve. Younger students may be more comfortable with class or teacher-led games. Older students prefer to work in smaller groups where they can contribute their opinions and express their thoughts and ideas to each other.*
- *Never ask a group to play a game you would not play yourself.*
- *Be very clear with your instructions. Ask for feedback from the students to make sure they understand what is involved and what each participant should do.*
- *Be enthusiastic. The students will be drawn to your energy and will get excited about the prospect of participating in the activity.*
- *Give a demonstration wherever possible.*
- *Involve yourself in the game. Don't give the group instructions and then go and sit in a corner of the room to watch or correct.*

Each drama game is listed with details of the minimum number of students required for the game to work. Detailed instructions are also provided with suggested extensions/variations for some of the games. The resources needed are included and the level of each game is described as follows:

- *Beginners+: suitable for all levels.*
- *Elementary+: suitable for all levels from elementary onwards.*
- *Pre-intermediate+: suitable for all levels from pre-intermediate onwards.*
- *Intermediate+: suitable for all levels from intermediate onwards.*

Getting-to-Know-You Activities

Getting-to-know-you games are a perfect opportunity for the students not only to learn their classmates' names but to also find out some interesting facts and information about them. Getting-to-know-you exercises should be fun and interactive. They help build trust and friendship among peers and lead to a happy and relaxed classroom environment. In addition, the activities in this section give the teacher some indication of the students' strengths and weaknesses in relation to the English language. The following aspects of language that are covered in this section include greetings, introductions, asking and answering questions, statements, present tense, gerunds, present perfect, adjectives and vocabulary.

Game: Greetings
Level: Beginners+
Other benefits: The focus of this game is for the students to learn how to greet people. The extension to the activity promotes imagination and creativity.
Minimum number of participants: 3
Resources needed: Clear space.
Instructions: The students stand up and walk around the room in different directions. They have 30 seconds to shake everyone's hand and say, "Hello, my name is …. Pleased to meet you."

Extension: You can make this more difficult for higher levels. Once the students have greeted everyone in 30 seconds, they can go around the room and greet everyone in different scenarios. The teacher calls out different scenarios.
Examples of different scenarios:
- *Greet someone you haven't seen for ten years.*
- *Greet someone who owes you money.*
- *Greet everyone as if they have bad breath.*
- *Greet everyone as if you are in love with them.*
- *Greet everyone as if you don't like them.*
- *Greet everyone as if you are suspicious of them.*
- *Greet everyone as if you are frightened of them*

Game: Snowballs
Level: Pre-intermediate+
Other benefits: Statements and interrogative questions are the language focus here, but this activity also helps the students to be observant and aware of other people's body language.
Minimum number of participants: 4
Resources needed: Clear space, pieces of paper and pens.
Instructions: This is a good icebreaker or warm-up game for a class that doesn't know each other that well. Give each student a piece of paper. Each student writes a statement about themselves on the piece of paper. When everyone has done this, they scrunch up the paper and throw it in the circle. They keep picking up and throwing different pieces of paper until the teacher says stop. They pick up a random piece of paper and they must ask each other questions to find out who the piece of paper belongs to. If the group knows each other well, get them to write down less obvious statements about themselves.

Game: Roll the Ball
Level: Beginners+
Other benefits: This is a very useful game to play at the start of a new class. It helps both the students and teacher learn each other's name in a fun way.
Minimum number of participants: 4
Resources needed: Clear space and a ball.
Instructions: This is a fun and easy game to play with younger students. It helps with coordination skills. You need a ball. All the students sit in a circle with their legs wide open. They say the following rhyme as they roll the ball to one another.
Roll the ball, roll the ball, roll the ball to (name)
(name) has got the ball, roll it back to me.

Game: Data Processing
Level: Elementary+
Other benefits: The main aim of this activity is to provide the students with the opportunity to ask each other personal questions. The game can also be used to develop listening skills.
Minimum number of participants: 4
Resources needed: Clear space.
Instructions: Get the class to work together and get them to get into a straight line:
- *Alphabetically by their first name*
- *Alphabetically by their surnames*
- *Alphabetically by their best friend's name*
- *By hair length*
- *By shoe size*
- *By birthdays*
- *By how many brothers and sisters you have*

Extension: If the students are more advanced, get them to do this exercise by not using sound. They can only use body movements and gestures.

Game: Action Name Game
Level: Beginners+
Other benefits: This is another effective but simple game to practice greetings and introductions. It also promotes awareness and teamwork skills.
Minimum number of participants: 4
Resources needed: Clear space.
Instructions: Have everyone sit in circle. The first student says, "Hi my name is ____" The student then does an action, and the rest of the group says, "Hi _____, pleased to meet you," and repeats the action. This continues until everyone has a chance and the rest of the group has greeted them and repeated their action.

Game: Adjective Introduction
Level: Beginners+
Other benefits: This is a good game for both learning classmates' names and practising adjectives.
Minimum number of participants: 2
Resources needed: Clear space, ball or a bean bag.
Instructions: The students form a circle and the teacher gives one of them a bean bag or a ball. When they have the ball/beanbag, they must introduce themselves and say an adjective that best describes them, for example "Hi, my name is Annie and I'm funny." When Annie is finished introducing herself, she throws the ball to someone else in the circle. This continues until everyone has had a turn.
Extension: To make this activity more difficult for more advanced students, the adjective they choose must start with the same letter as their name. Example, "Hi, I'm Annie and I'm awesome."

Game: Find Someone Who?
Level: Elementary+
Other benefits: This exercise mainly focuses on asking and answering questions. Examples of gerunds and the present perfect are below.
Minimum number of participants: 4
Resources needed: Clear space, pens and paper.
Instructions: This icebreaker activity requires students to form questions properly using a prompt. The teacher can create a worksheet based on prompts or she can write the prompts on the board. In order, to complete the activity, students must speak to a wide variety of students in the classroom, making this an excellent communication and listening game.

Example 1: To practice gerunds.

Question: Do you like/enjoy/love dancing?
Answer: Yes, I do. Yes, I like dancing.
Answer: No, I don't. No, I don't enjoy dancing.

Find Someone Who?
- *Likes dressing up*
- *Like eating*
- *Likes travelling*
- *Likes going to school*
- *Likes going out*
- *Likes playing*
- *Likes reading*
- *Likes meeting their friends*

Example 2: To practice the present perfect.
Question: Have you ever been to America?
Answer: Yes, I have. Yes, I have been to America.
Answer: No, I haven't. No, I've never been to America.

Find Someone Who?
- *Has read a book in last month*
- *Has gone to the cinema in the last week*
- *Has eaten a snail*
- *Has eaten raw fish*
- *Has been chased by a dog*
- *Has been to more than two schools*
- *Has seen a lion*
- *Has been to more than 10 countries in Europe*

Game: Pair Interviews
Level: Elementary+
Other benefits: This game helps with listening skills and gives the students practice in forming questions in the present tense.
Minimum number of participants: 2
Resources needed: Clear space.
Instructions: Divide the class into pairs. Each student must interview their partner. They must find out the following five things about them.

- *Name*
- *Nationality*
- *Age*
- *Siblings*
- *Favourite colour*

The questions can be more difficult depending on the students' level of English. Give the pairs a few minutes to complete the interviews. When they have completed this part of the task, each pair takes a turn standing up and introducing their partner to the rest of the class.

Extension: Everyone stands in a circle and the teacher throws a ball/ beanbag to a student and says a fact about them they have learned from listening to the introductions. The student then must throw the ball to another student calling out a fact about them and so on until everyone has had a chance at catching and throwing the ball.

Game: Three Truths and a Lie
Level: Pre-Intermediate+
Other benefits: This game helps the students to get to know each other better by giving them an opportunity to answer questions. This activity also encourages the students to use their imagination.
Minimum number of participants: 3
Resources needed: Pens and paper.
Instructions: Give each student a piece of paper and a pen. The students divide their sheet of paper into four sections. In three of the sections, they must write down true facts about themselves, and in the fourth, they must write down a lie. The rest of the class asks them questions to try to guess which statements are true and which one is the lie. The truths/lie can be very simple or very elaborate. It is up to each student to decide.

Game: Rainbow

Level: Beginners+

Other benefits: This game can be used to practice colours. This is a variation of the well-known drama activity "Fruit Basket." This game not only helps the student to physically warm up but it is an excellent listening and observation game.

Minimum number of participants: 7

Resources needed: Clear space and a chair for each student; if you do not have chairs, you can use sheets of paper or cushions.

Instructions: All the students sit in circle on a chair or a cushion. The teacher chooses three different colours and goes around the circle giving each person the name of a colour, in an order, for example, red, yellow, blue. A student is then chosen, or volunteers, to go into the centre of the circle. His/her chair is taken away. The student in the centre calls out the name of one of the three colours. If the student in the centre says red, then all the reds change places; if s/he says yellow, all the yellows change places, and if s/he says blue, all the blues change places. If s/he says rainbow, then everyone changes places. The student who is left without a chair, goes into the centre for the next round.

Variations: There are lots of variations to this game and you can change the names to go with a specific theme. The colours could be replaced by:

- *Fruit basket: apple, orange, and banana.*
- *Barnyard: chicken, pig and cow.*
- *Zoo: elephant, giraffe and tiger.*
- *Circus: clown, ringmaster and acrobat.*
- *Ocean: fish, mermaid and shark.*

Listening Activities

These activities promote active listening skills among young learners. They help them follow instructions and directions and make them aware of the importance of what other people say. Good listening skills improve both attention and concentration. Countable and uncountable nouns, directions, negatives, vocabulary development, question formation, action verbs, auxiliary verbs and speech sounds are the main language focus in this section.

Game: Shopping List
Level: Beginners+
Other benefits: The aim of this game is to extend shopping vocabulary, to practice, basic countable and uncountable nouns and focus on articulation.
Minimum number of participants: 6
Resources needed: A clear space and shopping lists.
Instructions: Ask for two volunteers: one is the mother and the other is the child. The mother leaves to go shopping but the child realises she forgot her shopping list. She runs out after her but she has already crossed the road. She shouts the contents of the list across the road and the mother takes it down. The road is very noisy as all the other students are the traffic. They must try to make as much noise as possible.
Example of the shopping list:
- *2 kilos of potatoes*
- *5 very large green peppers*
- *A single layer celebration cake*
- *A tube of toothpaste*
- *A packet of biscuits*
- *A dozen eggs*
- *A jar of peanut butter*

Game: The Fishing Game
Level: Elementary+
Other benefits: The focus of this game is to practice directions. It will also help students to become familiar with different types of fish.
Minimum number of participants: 4
Resources needed: Clear space.
Instructions: The students sit in a circle. The teacher goes around the circle and gives each student a fish name, such as a dog fish, sun fish, starfish, and catfish. Then, the teacher chooses one type of fish and the students that are assigned that fish move around the outside of the circle to instructions like "high seas" (stretching as high as they can), "low seas" (crouching as low as they can), and "choppy seas" (jumping or hopping, changing direction). When the teacher calls "shark is coming," they must run back as quickly as they can to their place in the circle. Repeat until all the fish have had a turn.

Game: World's Greatest Sandwich
Level: Elementary+
Other benefits: This is an excellent concentration and memory game. It will help to extend and explore vocabulary.
Minimum number of participants: 2
Resources needed: Clear space.
Instructions: This activity can be used as a getting-to-know-you activity as well as giving the students an opportunity to practice specific vocabulary. The students sit in a circle and the first-person starts.
Student A: Hi my name is Adam and the world's greatest sandwich has eggs in it.
Student B: Hi my name is Betty and the world's greatest sandwich has eggs and bananas in it.
Student C: Hi my name is Carol and the world's greatest sandwich has eggs, bananas and pickles in it.
Everyone in the circle gets a chance. If they make a mistake or pause too long, they are out. The game keeps going until there is only one person left.
Extension: This game could be used to practice other types of vocabulary.
Examples:
- *The world greatest zoo has .... (zoo animals)*
- *The world's greatest rainbow has .... (colours)*
- *The world greatest orchestra has .... (musical instruments)*

Game: I Like but I Don't Like
Level: Beginners+
Other benefits: This game helps to promote the students' creativity. It also focuses on negatives.
Minimum number of participants: 3
Resources needed: Clear space.
Instructions: Go around the circle and each student says what they like and what they don't like. You can make it more difficult by getting them to say items that start with the first letter of their name.
For example: *Hi my name is Julie. I like jellies but I don't like jam.*
After everyone has had a chance to say what their likes and dislikes are, the students stand in a circle. A volunteer is chosen and he calls out the name of another student across the circle. As he walks towards them, he must call out their likes and dislikes. The chosen student chooses someone else and walks towards them calling out their likes and dislikes and so on until everyone has had a turn.

Game: I'm Going on Holidays and I'm Going to Pack
Level: Elementary+
Other benefits: This game makes students aware of the alphabet and the sounds each letter makes. It develops imagination as well as vocabulary.
Minimum number of participants: 3
Resources needed: Clear space.
Instructions: The whole class sits in a circle. Each student must say that they are going on holidays and they are going to take two items with them. The first item must start with the first letter of their first name. The next item must begin with the first letter of their surname. If you want to make it more complicated, the items could be the last letter of their names. Everyone must listen carefully because at the end, each student must go around the group and say what everyone is bringing on holidays with them.

Game: Favourite Things
Level: Beginners+
Other benefits: This can also be used as a fun getting-to-know-you game. It can be used to extend and practice different vocabulary.
Minimum number of participants: 6
Resources needed: Clear space.
Instructions: The whole class spreads themselves randomly around the room. The teacher calls out a category question, for example, what is your favourite animal? All the students move around the room calling out their favourite animal and find other students in the class who have the same favourite animal as them. When a student finds another student, who has the same answer as them, they join and continue to go around the group looking for more students with the same answer. After sixty seconds, the teacher shouts "FREEZE." Each group needs to call out their answer. If there are two groups who have the same answer but are not joined together, they are eliminated from the next round.
Suggestions:
- *Favourite sport*
- *Favourite ice cream flavour*
- *Favourite TV show*
- *Favourite song*
- *Favourite colour*

Game: Group Connection
Level: Elementary+
Other benefits: An effective game for developing cohesion in a group, encouraging students to share information and form questions.
Minimum number of participants: 8
Resources needed: Clear space.
Instructions: The students walk casually around the room. The teacher instructs them to get into different types of groups; the groups can be varied. Use numbers such as groups of 3 or groups of students with the same colour hair, students born in the same month, born in the same country, same star sign, same year. The students can come up with ideas for other information they may wish to share with one another.

Game: Life Stories
Level: Pre-intermediate+
Other benefits: This game helps to explore narratives and practice reported speech such as, "You said...she said..."
Minimum number of participants: 4
Resources needed: Clear space, pens and paper (optional).
Instructions: The class is divided into pairs. Each student recounts an incident that happened in their lives. It can be specific incidents that made them feel...
- *Happy*
- *Sad*
- *Embarrassed*
- *Frightened*
- *Surprised*

After they have told the incident to one another, they join another pair. Each student gets a chance to tell their partner's story to the other pair. At the end, the students give feedback to one another about how accurately they recounted the story. The students can write down some points to help them remember.

Game: I Spy (Sound)
Level: Beginners+
Other benefits: The main aim of this game is to explore sounds made in the English language and to focus on English pronunciation.
Minimum number of participants: 2
Resources needed: A variety of objects in the room.
Instructions: One student volunteers to be it. They look around the room and say, "I spy with my little eye something that begins with the sound of "duh." The rest of the group must guess the object. They must listen carefully to the sound that is being made. Everyone in the group should have a turn being the leader.

Game: Bean Bag Action
Level: Elementary+
Other benefits: This game practices action verbs and helps students with their balance and coordination skills.
Minimum number of participants: 1
Resources needed: Clear space, bean bags or alternatives.
Instructions: Each student puts a bean bag on their head. If bean bags aren't available, get cushions, books, plastic cups, etc. Everyone balances the bean bags on their head. The teacher shouts out a series of actions. The students must see if they can do the action with the bean bag on their heads.
Action verbs suggestions:
- *Jump*
- *Run*
- *Skip*
- *Hop*
- *Walk*
- *Crawl*
- *Twist*
- *Kick*
- *Pull*
- *Bend*
- *Gallop*
- *Tip toe*
- *Push leap*
- *Stop*
- *Wiggle*
- *Climb*
- *Shake*
- *Twirl*
- *Throw*

Communication Activities

Communication drama games have a vital role to play in the ESL classroom. These activities help the learners to speak with and listen to other learners. The purpose of the following activities is for the students to find information, break down barriers and talk about themselves in a relaxed manner. The language areas that are practiced in this section are questions, conditionals, past and present simple tenses, past and present continuous tenses, there is/there are, expressions for giving opinions and negotiating.

Game: The Dog Show
Level: Pre-Intermediate+
Other benefits: This activity allows the students to practice forming questions and responding in an appropriate manner.
Minimum number of participants: 2
Resources needed: Clear space.
Instructions: This is a communication activity where the students must use their imagination. This is an opportunity for the students to use mime, providing a chance to use the "teacher in role" drama technique. Get each student to imagine that they are a dog owner. They must each mime interacting with their dog. Once they have done this and gotten used to the size of their dog, get them to imagine they are competing in a dog show. The teacher takes on the role as a judge of the show. She/he interviews each of the dog owners individually and asks them the following questions:

* *What type of dog is it?*
* *Where did you get him from?*
* *What type of personality does he have?*
* *What dog tricks can he do? Can you show us?*
* *Why should your dog win the show?*

The judge/teacher can decide at the end of the activity who wins the show. The winner/winners can take a photo at the end with their dogs. This is a still image (see Drama Techniques section).

Game: If I Were an Animal
Level: Pre-Intermediate+
Other benefits: The language focus of this game is to practice the conditional tense.
Minimum number of participants: 4
Resources needed: Clear space.
Instructions: Everyone sits in a circle and one by one each student says, "If I were an animal, I would be a _____" and then states a reason.
For example, "If I were an animal, I would be a lion because a lion is big and strong."
Then you could go around the circle again using the following:

* *If I were a car, I would be ....*
* *If I were a kitchen utensil, I would be ....*
* *If I were a sport, I would be ....*
* *If I were a country, I would be ....*
* *If I were a hobby, I would be....*
* *If I were a flower, I would be ....*
* *If I were an item of clothing, I would be.......*
* *If I were a body part, I would be.......*

Game: Alibi
Level: Pre-intermediate+
Other benefits: This game focuses on question formation as well as practising communicating in a spontaneous manner.
Minimum number of participants: 6
Resources needed: Clear space.
Instructions: Explain what an alibi means. Create a crime scene scenario. Divide the class into groups of 4 or 5. Get one group to be the suspects and send them out of the room to get their story straight. While the suspects are getting their story straight, get the other group to be the investigators. They must compile a series of questions. After the students are finished preparing their questions, invite the suspects back and the interrogation begins. Each group interviews each suspect and then they compare notes and decide whose story didn't match up; they must come to a consensus on who they will officially accuse.
Different scenarios:
  * *Bank robbery*
  * *Kidnapping*
  * *Shoplifting*

Extension: More advanced students could hold a trial in which each group is assigned different roles.

Game: Picture Starters
Level: Elementary+
Other benefits: This game also focuses on the present continuous tense as well as there is/there are.
Minimum number of participants: 4
Resources needed: Clear space and a variety of pictures.
Instructions: Gather a collection of pictures from magazines books, postcards or from the Internet; make sure there are enough pictures for everyone in the class. Place them face down and get each student to choose one. Give them time to observe the card. In a circle, each student must share what they can about the picture, such as…
What is happening in the picture?
What feelings/emotions does the picture make you think about?

Extension: Divide the students into groups. They choose a picture and they recreate the picture by using a still image (see Drama Techniques section). The picture can come to life and dialogue can be used for more advanced students.

Game: Air, Earth, Fire, Water
Level: Elementary+
Other benefits: This is a fun and imaginative game that helps build vocabulary.
Minimum number of participants: 4
Resources needed: Clear space.
Instructions: The students stand in a circle. The teacher throws the ball. If the teacher says earth, the student who catches the ball must say the name of an animal on earth. The rest of the group must move around the room and sound like the chosen animal.

If the teacher says air, the student who catches the ball must say the name of any bird in the air. The rest of the group must move around the room and sound like the chosen animal.

If the teacher says water, the student who catches the ball must say the name of anything that lives in water. The rest of the group must move around the room and sound like the chosen animal.

If the teacher says fire, the student who catches must say the name of something you can burn. The rest of the group must sculpt themselves into the shape of the object.

If someone makes a mistake or gets it wrong, they are out.

Game: Penny for Your Thoughts
Level: Beginners+
Other benefits: This is a creative game to practice the simple past tense and the past continuous tense.
Minimum number of participants: 4
Resources needed: Clear space and a selection of pennies with different years on them. The pennies can either be real or made before the class begins.
Instructions: Give a penny to each member of the class. The dates on the pennies must correspond with the ages of the students, so if most of the class was born in 2000 then the dates of the pennies should be 2000 to 2016. Divide the class into groups of four and each student in the group tells the rest of the group what they were doing the year that is stamped on their penny. After each student, has finished, they exchange pennies and form a new group. You can do this for three or four rounds and get everyone speaking.

Game: Desert Island
Level: Pre-Intermediate+
Other benefits: This game develops negotiation and listening skills. Expressions for giving opinions are practiced.
Minimum number of participants: 4
Resources needed: Clear space and pens and paper.
Instructions: This can be a whole class activity or it can be done in smaller groups. It is excellent for team building and very good for developing communication skills. Tell the class they are on a boat that is sinking. They see a desert island in the distance and they can save the following items from the boat.
Items:

- *A box of matches*
- *A rope*
- *A sewing kit*
- *A crate of coke*
- *An inflatable raft*
- *A bottle opener*
- *An axe*
- *A compass*
- *A pocket knife*
- *50 jars of peanut butter*
- *A first aid kit*
- *A signal flare*
- *A razor blade*
- *A torch*
- *A mobile phone*
- *A tent*
- *10 blankets*
- *10 pillows*
- *12 rolls of toilet paper*
- *A guitar*
- *A bottle of whiskey*

Individually, the students must rank the items in order of importance from one to twenty, with one being the most important item and twenty the least important item. Divide the class into groups of four/five; each group must come up with a group consensus from one to twenty in order of importance. The group provides feedback to the teacher. Did the group discussion change anybody's individual opinion? Does each member think the group's order of importance is the best or do they think their own individual importance is better?

Game: Object Sculpting
Level: Beginners+
Other benefits: Target specific language and form simple questions.
Minimum number of participants: 4
Resources needed: Clear space.
Instructions: Divide the class into pairs (A & B). "A" becomes the sculptor and "B" becomes the clay. Tell each pair that 'A' is going to mould 'B' into an object from a category that the teacher calls out, for example:

- *Fruit*
- *Transport*
- *Kitchen utensil*
- *Body part*
- *Musical instrument*
- *Toy*
- *Superhero*

When they are finished, all the 'A's go around and look at the different clay pieces and must guess what type of object they are. When this is finished, 'B' becomes the sculptor and 'A' the clay.

Game: Going on a Journey
Level: Elementary+
Other benefits: This game explores the students' imagination and helps to practice the past tense and describing places.
Minimum number of participants: 4
Resources needed: Clear space.
Instructions: Divide the class into groups. Each group decides where they are going. They discuss what they need. Students pack their bags. They create a freeze frame (see Drama Techniques section) where they are going. When the teacher says go, they begin their journey. When the teacher says stop, groups are mixed up and in pairs they describe their journey and where they have been.

Game: Guess Who?

Level: Pre-Intermediate+

Other benefits: This is an enjoyable game where students must listen carefully. The game helps students practice the present tense and question formation.

Minimum number of participants: 8

Resources needed: Clear space, cards with the names of famous people on them, pen and paper for each student (autograph book).

Instructions: Each student is given a name of a well-known person. They must keep it a secret from everyone else. They then go to a party and they talk to the other well-known people at the party. They can't reveal who they are but they can answer questions. Once a student has guessed correctly, they must get the autograph of the well-known person. The winner is the one with the most autographs on their page at the end.

Suggestions:
- *Madonna*
- *Donald Trump*
- *Nelson Mandela*
- *Mother Teresa*
- *Bill Gates*
- *Walt Disney*
- *Dalai Lama*
- *Lionel Messi*
- *Harry Potter*
- *William Shakespeare*
- *Justin Bieber*
- *Taylor Swift*
- *Miley Cyrus*
- *The Queen*
- *The Pope*

Co-Operative Activities

Cooperative activities help to develop students' ability to work successfully in a group. This process enables ESL students to improve patience, socialisation and their capacity to problem-solve. These activities are very effective in ESL settings as they provide the students with an opportunity to actively listen to one another and articulate their thoughts and ideas in a clear manner. The following activities help ESL students to be a valuable part of a team, which helps to promote confidence and self-esteem, as it gives them the opportunity to demonstrate their skills and abilities. Parts of speech, adjectives, verbs, numbers, sequencing skills, alphabet, vocabulary, rhyme, instructions and directions are the main language skills explored and practiced in this section.

Game: Mixed-up Sentences
Level: Beginners+
Other benefits: This interactive and enjoyable game helps the students to practice different parts of speech.
Minimum number of participants: 8
Resources needed: Clear space and 8 boxes with the different parts of speech clearly labelled on them.
Instructions: Divide the class into groups; label 8 boxes with a part of speech.

- *Parts of speech*
- *Noun*
- *Pronoun*
- *Adjective*
- *Adverb*
- *Preposition*
- *Conjunction*
- *Interjection*

Each group comes up with an appropriate word to put in each of the labelled boxes. They choose words from the different boxes and they put them into a grammatical correct sentence, even if the sentence is nonsense. Each group must act out the sentence for the other groups by using expressive movement.

Game: Combination Game
Level: Elementary+
Other benefits: Adjectives are the main language focus of this game.
Minimum number of participants: 4
Resources needed: Clear space.
Instructions: The whole class sits in a circle. The teacher says the name of an object and the student next to her must give an adjective that describes that object. They then say an object and the student next to them says an adjective to describe their object. Everyone in the circle gets an opportunity to say an object and describe an object by using an adjective.

Game: Stop the Bus
Level: Elementary+
Other benefits: This game is a simple and effective way to practise English language sounds and build vocabulary.
Minimum number of participants: 4
Resources needed: Clear space, whiteboard, whiteboard markers.
Instructions: Divide the class into small groups of three or four. The teacher will call out a category and a letter/sound. The first group to run to the white board with a word from the category starting with the letter/sound gets five points. An example is, if the teacher called out, "Fruits and B," the first group to run up and write bananas would get five points. Each group gets a point for each letter in their word if it is spelt correctly. When the groups have completed writing their word on the board, they shout, "Stop the Bus." Words cannot be repeated.
Suggested categories:
- *Girl names*
- *Boy names*
- *Fruits*
- *Sports*
- *Colours*
- *Animals*
- *Occupations*
- *Countries*
- *Transport*
- *Birds*
- *Pets*
- *Sweets*
- *Chocolates*
- *TV shows*
- *Fairy tales*
- *Superheroes*
- *Cartoons*

Game: Twenty to One
Level: Beginners+
Other benefits: The students work as part of a group to reach a goal. This is also an excellent game to use to improve reactions and to practice numbers.
Minimum number of participants: 5
Resources needed: Clear space.
Instructions: The group sits in a circle. Get the students to count from one to twenty together. The students must count to twenty, with one student saying one number at a time. One student volunteers to start counting. Any of the other students can say the next number; however, the count stops if two or more students speak at the same time. Then the students must restart the count. If everyone works together as a team, the group can reach twenty very quickly. More advanced students can try this game by counting in reverse from twenty to one.

Game: Where Are We?
Level: Elementary+
Other benefits: This game helps students to stimulate their imagination and practice their sequencing skills.
Minimum number of participants: 8
Resources needed: Clear space, bench or chairs.
Instructions: Place a bench or a row of chairs at the front of the classroom. Divide the class into groups of four. The teacher informs the students that they are spectators of a specific event. Each group must choose their event. Each group is allowed five minutes to discuss and practice being spectators at their event. When the students are ready, each group takes turns to come to the front of the class and mime watching the event. The rest of the class must guess the event that group is watching. To make it more difficult for more advanced groups, they must start speaking, adding words that match their actions.
Suggested Events:
- *An MMA fight*
- *A horror film*
- *A tennis match*
- *A beauty pageant*
- *A weightlifting competition*
- *A bull fight*
- *A motorbike race*
- *A music concert*
- *A comic show*
- *A funny play*

Game: Human Alphabet
Level: Beginners+
Other benefits: This game will help students review the alphabet and spelling in an active way.
Minimum number of participants: 4
Resources needed: Clear space.
Instructions: The class is divided into pairs. The teacher calls out a letter of the alphabet and each pair has ten seconds to make that letter with their bodies. After a while, two pairs join to make groups of four. The teacher calls out two- or three- letter words and the group of four must make the words with their bodies. If there are enough students in the class, two groups of four can join to make a group of eight and they can make larger words.

Game: Sixty-Second Rhyming Race
Level: Elementary+
Other benefits: This is an imaginative and interactive way to practice rhyme.
Minimum number of participants: 4
Resources needed: Clear space and cards with words on them.
Instructions: Divide the class into groups of four. One student volunteers from each group. The volunteers choose a word from the stack of cards. The volunteer must mime as many words that rhyme with their chosen word in sixty seconds. The rest of their group must guess the words. They get a point for each correct guess. When the sixty seconds is completed, another student from the group takes a different card and the process continues. The group with the most points by the end of the game wins.
Suggested words:
- *Bite*
- *My*
- *Sip*
- *Wake*
- *Hot*
- *Row*
- *Red*
- *Fun*
- *Sat*
- *Shoe*
- *Phone*
- *Book*
- *Pen*
- *But*
- *Deep*

Game: Action Charades
Age: Elementary+
Other benefits: This is an ideal way to practise verbs.
Minimum number of participants: 4
Resources needed: Clear space and a list of verbs.
Instructions: If there is a large number, of students, divide them into groups of 4 or 5. Give each group a verb, such as clean, cook or swim. One student will mime the verb to their group. The group members have a minute or two to guess the verb. To reduce noise, have one group participate at a time, while the other group members watch.
Suggestions of Verbs:
- *Taste*
- *Smell*
- *Dance*
- *Jog*
- *Skate*
- *Scream*
- *Fight*
- *Cry*
- *Read*
- *Write*
- *Cook*
- *Clean*
- *Paint*
- *Joke*
- *Sleep*
- *Sneeze*

Game: Poison Ivy
Level: Elementary+
Other Benefits: This also works very well as a listening game. The students get an opportunity to practise giving and receiving instructions and directions.
Minimum number of participants: 6
Resources needed: Clear space, a blindfold (optional).
Instructions: The teacher chooses one student to be a rescuer and another student to be the person who is lost. The rest of the students are poison ivy bushes. Tell them to find somewhere to sit in the clear space and spread out. Their arms are branches that can move in the breeze, but they cannot move from their place. The student who is lost must close their eyes, or if they want, they can be blindfolded. Tell them it is late at night and they have wandered into a forest of poison ivy. If they touch a plant or the plant touches them, they will be poisoned and die. The rescuer must guide the lost student from one end of the poison ivy forest to the other, but they can only use verbal instructions. The objective of the game is for the rescuer to guide the lost student from one end of the forest to the other, without being touched by the poison ivy. The lost student must listen very carefully to the instructions. If the lost student dies, then another pair gets the chance to be the lost student and the rescuer.

Game: Master and Robots
Level: Elementary+
Other Benefits: The students work as part of a pair practicing how to give clear directions to their partners.
Minimum number of participants: 2
Resources needed: Clear space.
Instructions: This is a fun game that students really enjoy. Divide the group into pairs. Student A is the master and Student B is the robot. The master must guide the robot around the clear space by giving them very specific directions. The masters can say: "Go ten steps forwards," or, "Put your hands in the air and turn around five times." The masters must make sure that their robot does not bump into other masters and robots in the group.

Concentration Activities

The following concentration activities help students with their observation skills. One of the benefits of these games is that they can be played in a restricted space. They help students to develop a sustained focus of the mind, body and voice, which also helps with general school life. The games in this section focus on vocabulary building and practice, questions, the alphabet, numbers, sounds and articulation, body parts, present and past tenses, comparatives, articles, nouns and descriptive words.

Game: Actions and Words
Level: Beginners+
Other benefits: This game builds on the student's vocabulary in a fun and memorable way.
Number of participants: 6
Resources needed: Clear space, cards with different words on them.
Instructions: The teacher decides on a category, e.g., sports. Each student is given a card with a different word based on the chosen category. Give the students thirty seconds to think of an action to accompany their word. Go around the circle as everyone says their word with the action. After everyone has shown their actions, have them pass random words to each other. The students must remember the action associated with the word. When a student performs the wrong action, they are eliminated. The category can be more difficult for more advanced students.
Suggestions of categories:
- *Food*
- *TV programmes*
- *Colours*
- *Superheroes*
- *Body parts*
- *Technology*
- *Objects found in a kitchen*
- *Objects found in a classroom*

Game: Back Talk
Level: Beginners+
Other benefits: This is a very simple game which focuses on the alphabet and practices target vocabulary.
Minimum number of participants: 6
Resources needed: Clear space and a list of words.
Instructions: Divide the class into two groups. Both groups stand in a line with their back to the person behind them. The teacher gives the students at the end of each group a simple word. They write that word with their finger on the back of the person in front of them.

Game: Number Line
Level: Beginners+
Other benefits: The focus of this game is to practice numbers and develop listening skills.
Number of participants: 10
Resources needed: A clear space.
Instructions: Divide the class into groups of ten. Each student has a number from 0-9 in each group. If you have only 8 in a group, number them from 0-7.

The teacher calls out a number and the students on each team who have been assigned part of that number must line up in correct order. The team who lines up first gets a point. The team with the most numbers at the end are winners.

Try these numbers or make up your own.

- *415*
- *136*
- *701*
- *248*
- *312*
- *973*
- *4,021*
- *1,234*
- *506, 789*
- *32,795*

Game: Lip Reading
Level: Beginners+
Other benefits: The main aim of this activity is to practice English language sounds and develop the students' articulation.
Number of participants: 10
Resources needed: Clear space.
Instructions: Divide the class into 2 groups. Each group numbers themselves from 1 to 10. The teacher gives each number 1 a simple word. They come out and mouth the word to number 2 who mouths the word to number 3 and so on until number 10 must guess the original word. The group who guesses the word correctly is the winner. The object is the student must think carefully how they use their organs of articulation. Organs of Articulation are the tongue, the teeth, the hard palate, the soft palate and the lips.

Game: How Do I Feel?
Level: Elementary+
Other benefits: This game focuses on body parts, present and past tenses, comparatives.
Minimum number of participants: 1
Resources needed: A clear space.
Instructions: The students all lie on the floor. Take deep breaths in. Get them to notice where they are tense. Shake out and relax their bodies. Then tense again and relax again.
Extension: Get them to describe how their bodies feel when it is tense and how it feels when they are relaxed; what's the difference.

Game: Statement Story
Level: Elementary+
Other benefits: The main aim of this game is to use the imagination; it gets the students to listen carefully to one another.
Minimum number of participants: 4
Resources needed: Clear space.
Instructions: Everyone sits in a circle. One student volunteers to makes a statement. The student next to the volunteer says a sentence that starts with the last word of the previous statement. For example, Student A says, "I am going to town." Student B says, "Town is busy." Student C says, "Busy people are busy with their shopping." Student D says, "Shopping is one of my favourite pastimes." Student E says, "Pastimes are important for relaxation." This can get very difficult as the statement story progresses around the circle.

Game: Generation game
Level: Elementary+
Other benefits: This is a fun and fast-paced game that stimulates the memory. The language focus is to practice articles and nouns.
Number of participants: 8
Resources needed: Clear space and list/pictures of objects.
Instructions: One student volunteers to be "it" and sits on a chair. The rest of the students are given a name/picture of an object. They must walk passed the student who is it and say the name of the object. The person who is it has two minutes to remember and list out all the objects. Each student should have an opportunity to sit in the chair.

Game: Three Changes
Level: Elementary+
Other benefits: This game practises vocabulary for personal descriptions as well as observation skills.
Number of participants: 2
Resources needed: Clear space.
Instructions: Divide the class into pairs. Each pair faces each other and looks at each other carefully for thirty seconds. They turn their backs to one another and they change three things about their appearance. When they are finished changing their appearance, they face each other again. They each must say out loud what the three differences are.

Game: Sound Script
Level: Pre-Intermediate+
Other benefits: This game focuses on the descriptive words for sounds and formatting questions.
Number of participants: 4
Resources needed: A clear space and cards with sounds on them.
Instructions: Each student chooses a card with a sound. They mustn't show any of the class. Go around the circle and each student makes their sound. The rest of the class must describe the sound and guess what sound was on the card. If they can't guess the sound, they can ask closed questions. The person making the sound can only answer yes or no to the questions asked.
Sound suggestions:
- *A dog barking*
- *A sheep bleating*
- *A bird chirping*
- *An owl hooting*
- *A bell ringing*
- *A balloon bursting*
- *A phone ringing*
- *A can spraying*
- *A horn beeping*
- *A drum banging*
- *A guitar strumming*
- *Some bacon sizzling*
- *Thunder clapping*
- *A baby crying*
- *A car crashing.*

Game: Which One Is Mine?
Level: Elementary+
Other benefits: This game practices descriptive words.
Number of participants: 6
Resources needed: A clear space and an orange for each student.
Instructions: Students work in large groups of 6 to 8. Each member of the group chooses an orange from a basket. The students must examine their orange very carefully. When they have finished examining the oranges, they put them back in the basket. The teacher mixes up the oranges and then each student takes it in turn to choose their orange. They must explain to the rest of the class why they think it is their original orange.

Imagination Activities

Games that stimulate students' imagination provide them with an opportunity to role-play different situations. The following games not only stimulate creativity but they enhance social skills and empathy, as they allow the students to imagine themselves in someone else's shoes. Imagination is an important building block for increasing self-esteem and confidence. It helps students to use their own initiative and gives them control over the world they have created. The main language aspects focused on in this section are vocal clarity, vocabulary related to emotions and feelings, modal verbs, language of persuasion, credibility and possibility, prepositions of place, opposites and homonyms, verbs related to the senses, gestures and the progressive tenses.

Game: Tricky Tongue Twisters 1
Level: Beginners+
Other benefits: This game is a fun way to improve the clarity of different sounds.
Minimum number of participants: 1
Resources needed: A clear space and a list of tongue twisters; see some examples below.
Instructions: The teacher chooses a tongue twister from the list below (under Tricky Tongue Twisters 2). Everyone moves around slowly. The teacher claps her hand and the students walk at a normal pace. When the teacher claps her hands, they go at a quicker pace. The teacher keeps clapping and the students keep getting faster.

Game: Tricky Tongue Twisters 2
Level: Elementary+
Other benefits: The focus of this game is to improve both vocal clarity and fluency.
Number of participants: 4
Resources needed: Clear space.
Instructions: Write a tongue twister on the board. For more advanced learners, give them a sound and get them to write their own tongue twisters on the board.
Divide the class into two groups. Give each group a piece of paper with an emotion on it. See list of emotions below.
Then put them in a scenario, such as they are waiting at the bus stop.
They have a conversation with one another but they just use the tongue twister.
They greet each other using that emotion.
They wait and look at the weather. They complain to one another using the tongue twister.
A bus comes and they flag it down, but it passes them.
It starts to rain.
A car comes and splashes them.
Eventually, the bus comes and picks them up.
The other groups look at the performance and at the end, they try to guess each other's emotion.

Some sample tongue-twisters to help you get started:
A skunk sat on a stump. The stump thought the skunk stunk. The skunk thought the stump stunk. What stunk? The skunk or the stump?

A tutor who tooted the flute, tried to tutor two tooters to toot; said the two tooters to the tutor: "Is it harder to toot or to tutor two tooters to toot?"

If Freaky Fred found fifty feet of fruit and fed forty feet to his friend Frank, how many feet of fruit did Freaky Fred find?

Pepperoni pizza on a pink-patterned plate with parsley on the side to your pleasure.

Peter Piper picked a peck of pickled peppers. If Peter Piper picked a peck of pickled peppers, where's the peck of pickled peppers Peter Piper picked?

Red Leather Yellow Leather Red Leather Yellow Leather Red Leather Yellow Leather...

She shut the shop shutters so the shopping shoppers can't shop.

Unique New York; Unique New York; Unique New York ...

Which wristwatch is a Swiss wristwatch?

I like New York, unique New York, I like unique New York.

Peggy Babcock loves Tubby Gig whip.

Two toads totally tired, tried to trot to Tewkesbury.

She stood upon the balcony, inimitably mimicking him hiccupping and amicably welcoming him in.

The sixth sick Sheik's sixth sheep's sick.

Betty Botter bought some butter, but she said, "This butter's bitter. But a bit of better butter's better than the bitter butter that would make my batter better." So, she bought some better butter better than the bitter butter And it made her batter better. So 'twas better Betty Botter, Bought a bit of better butter.

Suggested Emotions:
- *Anger*
- *Happy*
- *Sad*
- *Disgust*
- *Surprise*
- *Fear*
- *Boredom*
- *Envy*
- *Love*
- *Lonely*
- *Pride*
- *Regret*
- *Shame*

Game: Emotional Orchestra
Level: Pre-Intermediate+
Other benefits: This game will help the students to explore emotions and feelings.
Minimum number of participants: 2
Resources needed: Clear space, pieces of paper with emotions on it.
Instructions: Each student in the group chooses a piece of paper with an emotion on it. You may need to pre-teach some of the vocabulary to make sure that everyone understands their emotion. (See list of emotions above.) Go around the group and ask each student to make a movement and a sound that is connected to their chosen emotion. When everyone has done that explain that you are going to be a conductor and when you count to three, you are going to conduct an emotional orchestra. Count to three and everyone makes their movement and their sound together. If the conductor raises their hands, the volume must go up; if the conductor puts their hands by their chest, then it should be a medium volume, and if the hands are by the waist, it should be low and quiet. The purpose of this exercise is to practice emotion and vocabulary and to get the students to use their imagination and creativity.

Extension:
This activity can be used to practice other vocabulary, such as:
- *Jungle Symphony – (Jungle animals)*
- *Kitchen Symphony – (Kitchen utensils)*
- *Transport Symphony – (Types of transport)*

Game: Call My Bluff
Level: Elementary+
Other benefits: This game focuses on the language of persuasion, credibility and possibility, including modal verbs.
Number of participants: 6
Resources needed: Clear space and a list of obscure words.
Instructions: Divide the class into two teams. Each team will be given a list of obscure and/or difficult words with which they are not yet familiar. They can look up the meaning in the dictionary. Each team prepares three definitions for each word – one is true, the other are made up by the students. Taking turns, the team writes its word on the board and then announces the three definitions. After a, given period, the opposing team must choose which definition they think is correct; if they are right, they are given a point. The team with the most points win in the end.

Game: Alien Visitor
Level: Pre-intermediate+
Other benefits: The focus of this game is to practice adjectives and adverbs.
Number of participants: 4
Resources needed: A clear space with lots of different objects.
Instructions: The teacher tells the students that he/she is an alien who has just arrived on earth. The alien can speak a very basic level of English but wants to learn more to teach other aliens back on his/her own planet. The aliens ask the students about an object in the room or something in general. The alien points at an object and says, "What's this?" the students will respond, "It's a desk." Then the alien says, "What's a desk?" The students must explain the desk or any other chosen object by talking about what it is used for, when and where to use it, where it is from.

Game: Five Senses
Level: Elementary+
Other benefits: To explore the five senses and focus on these verbs: to listen, to watch, to see, to look, to taste, to smell, to touch.
Number of participants: 1
Resources needed: A clear space.
Instructions: Each student must show the sense using facial expressions and body language that are…
  • *Listening to the teacher.*
  • *Looking at a horror film.*
  • *Tasting some delicious food.*
  • *Touching something soft.*
  • *Smelling something very nasty.*
Get each student to choose a sense and a situation and the rest of class must pose in the suggested way.

Game: Inanimate Voices
Level: Elementary+
Other benefits: The main aims of this activity are prepositions of place, vocabulary practice, and feelings.
Number of participants: 4
Resources needed: Clear space.
Instruction: Get the students to find a space in the room. The teacher tells them to focus, look around the room in silence and examine all the objects in the room very carefully. Then, the students must choose an object. They have 10 seconds to make the shape of the inanimate object. Everyone freezes in the shape of their object. The teacher goes around the room and taps each object on the shoulder. Each object must speak in character. For example, a chair may say, "I'm so tired; if one more person sits on me, I will cry."

Extension 1: To develop and extend vocabulary, the teacher can introduce different categories. The students could become an object that is found…

- *In the kitchen*
- *In the bedroom*
- *In the car*
- *In a handbag*
- *In a sitting room*
- *At a party*
- *At a friend's house*
- *At a disco*
- *In a toy shop*
- *On the road*
- *At the beach*

Extension 2: To extend this activity further, get the students to write monologues with inanimate objects as the character. A monologue is a short scene with just one character talking. The students can perform their monologues for one another.

Game: Opposites
Level: Beginners+
Other benefits: To practice opposites and homonyms.
Number of participants: 2
Resources needed: Clear space and a list of antonyms/homonyms.
Instructions: Divide the class into pairs. The teacher calls out a word and Student A must mime the word. Student B must mime the opposite meaning. Alternate the rounds so that each student gets a chance of miming the word and the opposite words.
Suggested Antonyms:
- *Alive/dead*
- *All/nothing*
- *Always/never*
- *Boy/girl*
- *Better/worse*
- *Common/rare*
- *Deep/shallow*
- *Few/many*
- *Heavy/light*
- *In/out*
- *Left/right*
- *Little/big*
- *Night/day*
- *On/off*
- *Sorrow/joy*
- *Up/down*

Extension: For more advanced students, you can use this activity to practice homonyms.

Game: Still Image Dictation
Level: Elementary+
Other benefits: This game practices simple, present and present progressive tenses.
Number of participants: 4
Resources needed: A clear space.
Instructions: Give each group a different scenario and give them a few minutes to come up with a still image to depict the scene. When each group is ready, get them to freeze in their still image at the top of the class. When each group is ready get them to freeze in their still image at the top of the class. The other groups describe the scene.

Game: Wizards, Giants and Goblins
Level: Beginners+
Other benefits: This game works well as warm-up game. It develops listening and reaction skills.
Number of participants: 6
Resources needed: Clear space.
Instructions: The teacher counts to three each number. The group takes a large step. On the third count, each student takes the position of one of the following characters:
Wizards: Lean forward throwing their arms forward as if casting a spell.
Giants: Hands up high and say, "Ho hi ho."
Goblins: Crouch down, put their hands up to their face as if scratching their beards and make a high-pitch laugh.
Giants beat wizards, wizards beat goblins and goblins beat giants. This activity can be used with different characters.

Game: Gestures
Level: Beginners+
Other benefits: The main aim of this activity is to practice gestures made in the English language.
Number of participants: 2
Resources needed: Clear space.
Instructions:
Use Western gestures in your class.
Expressions/Gestures
Hello/wave
Goodbye/wave
It's cold/put arms around shoulders
It's hot/fan your face with hands
No!/Shake your head "no"
Come here/move your index finger
Me!/Touch your chest
OK/make the OK sign
I don't know/pull shoulders and hands up
Quiet/index finger in front of mouth
Stop/hand up, palm out
Stand up/raise hand slightly, palm up
Sit down/lower hand slightly, palm down
Once the students understand and have practiced the gestures and their meaning, divide the class into groups of three. Each group must come up with a sentence that they can use three of the above gestures. They perform their sentence to the other groups.

Extension: For more advanced groups, they can use the gestures to develop an improvisation that they can perform for the rest of the class.

Movement Activities

Movement is an essential part of drama and is the focus of this section of the book. The activities have been chosen specifically because they are fun and enjoyable. The activities allow the ESL students to practice some elements of the English language, such as target vocabulary, shapes, emotions, present simple, present continuous, verbs, prepositions, language sequencing and vowel letters and sounds. In addition to this, movement promotes group cohesion and trust, increases self-confidence and awareness and affords the ESL students the opportunity to express themselves creatively.

Game: Guess the Animal
Level: Beginners+
Other benefits: This activity helps the students practice both vocabulary and the present simple tense. It also develops the imagination.
Minimum number of participants: 4
Resources needed: A clear space, pictures of animals or pieces of paper with different animals written on them.
Instructions: Get each student to think of an animal, or the teacher can give them a piece of paper with the name of an animal on it. If they are complete beginners, you can give them a picture of an animal. Each student takes the opportunity to:
  • *Move like their animal*
  • *Make the sound of their animal*
  • *Describe their animal*
Example: Describing a lion, they could say, "He lives in the jungle. He roars and he eats other animals."

Game: Substitution
Level: Beginners+
Other benefits: Vowels letters and sounds and practicing target vocabulary are some the benefits of this game.
Minimum number of participants: 2
Resources needed: Clear space and a white/black board.
Instructions: This is an excellent activity to practice new vocabulary. Write a series of words on the board. The words could be related to a category or they could be new vocabulary that they have just learned.
If the word they read has an…
A – They slap their hands
E – They turn around
I – They jump up and down
O- They sit up down and stand up
U – They hop on one leg.
If the words have more than one vowel letter, they must do all the actions.

Game: What's in the Box?
Level: Beginners+
Other benefits: This game builds vocabulary and practices the present continuous tense.
Minimum number of participants: 4
Resources needed: Clear space.
Instructions: Get the group to sit in a circle. Get the students to imagine that there is a box in the centre of the circle. One by one they take turns opening the box. They each take an object of their choice out of the box. They mime using their chosen object to the group. The rest of the group must guess what the object is. They can do so by asking questions. For example, if someone takes out a television from the box, the others can ask, "Are you watching television?"

Game: Prepositional String
Level: Elementary+
Other benefits: This activity will help the students to understand the prepositions of place.
Minimum number of participants: 2
Resources needed: A clear space and a piece of string for each pair.
Instructions: Divide the class into pairs and give each pair a piece of string. Get each pair to show how you could use the piece of string as anything other than a piece of string.
Examples:
  • *A tight rope*
  • *A swimming pool*
  • *A fishing rod*

As the groups show their different uses of the pieces, the teacher and the other students ask the students where they are in relationship to each object that they made with the piece of string.

Examples:
  • *On*
  • *Around*
  • *Beside*
  • *In front of*
  • *At the back, of*
  • *In*
  • *At*

Game: Movement Sequences
Level: Elementary+
Other benefits: This game focuses on sequencing language, such as first, next, before that, afterwards. It helps to practice verbs of movement and to put the past simple tense into practice.
Minimum number of participants: 2
Requirements: Clear space.
Instructions: The teacher discusses with the students the different ways we can move. Elicit as many verbs from them to express the way people move.
See the suggestions below for different ways to move:

- *Walking*
- *Running*
- *Crawling*
- *Rolling*
- *Hopping*
- *Skipping*
- *Jumping*
- *Leaping*
- *Tiptoeing*
- *Tumbling*
- *Turning*
- *Galloping*
- *Twirling*
- *Spinning*
- *Walking sideways*
- *Walking backwards*

Divide the class into groups of three. Each group must come up with their own movement sequence. Each group should have at least five or six different movements. Each group then performs their movement sequence for the rest of class. The rest of the class must look at them carefully and recall their sequence. For example, they could say, "**First** you walked and **next** you galloped; **after that** you tumbled but **before** the tumble, you twirled and **at the same time** you jumped."

Game: Alphabet Verb
Level: Elementary+
Other benefits: This is a vocabulary-builder activity with a specific focus on verbs.
Minimum number of participants: 6
Resources needed: A clear space.
Instructions: Divide the class into groups of threes. The students must come up with one verb for each letter of the alphabet. As a group, they are given time to write down the verbs. When the groups have completed the task, they must perform the verbs through movement to the other group/s. Each group receives a point if they have a different verb than the other group/s. If two groups have the same verb, they don't receive a point. The teacher keeps track of the score on the board. The group with the most points wins the game.
Scaled version: If the students are not that advanced, the teacher can give the groups one letter at a time. This will make it easier for them.

Game: What Are You Doing?
Level: Elementary+
Other benefits: This is a very good activity to practice the present continuous and vocabulary.
Minimum number of participants: 4
Resources needed: A clear space.
Instructions: Divide the class into two groups. The groups form vertical lines facing the teacher. The first student in line A starts an activity such as digging a hole, knitting a jumper, or brushing their hair. The first student from line B asks, "What are you doing?" While the first student from line, A continues to dig a hole, he says, "I'm washing my car." The student from line B must immediately start washing his car while the first student goes to the back of the line and the next student moves up. The student who just moved up asks, "What are you doing?" Again, the other student in front must continue to wash a car while he says, for example, "I'm brushing my hair." This goes on until all the students have had a chance. If students hesitate, freeze up or stop what they are doing while they say what they are doing, they are eliminated from the game. The last student standing is the winner of the game.

Game: Instructions
Level: Beginners+
Other benefits: This game helps the students to understand instructions, follow instructions and improve listening skills.
Minimum number of participants:
Resources needed: A clear space and a white board.
Instructions: The teacher writes the following instructions on the whiteboard. When she calls out the following commands, the students must do the following actions.

Commands	Actions
Wall	place two hands on the wall
Middle	run to the centre of the room
Jump	jump twice and walk.
Hop	hop on one leg and stand still
Stop	freeze
Go	move at a normal pace
Slow	walk in slow motion
Fast	run

Extension 1: Once the students have gotten used to the instructions, the teacher can erase them from the board.

Extension 2: Reverse the instructions. For example, stop means go and fast means slow.

Game: Pass the Smile Around
Level: Beginners+
Minimum number of participants: 3
Other benefits: This game introduces the students to different types of emotions.
Resources: Clear space
Instructions: The game begins with everyone sitting in a circle. Student A smiles at everyone around the circle, trying to make someone else giggle or laugh. He gets a point for everyone who can't keep a totally straight face. After a while, he uses one hand to literally "wipe" the smile off his face, and hand it to the student next to him in the circle. This activity can be more difficult for more advanced students. Instead of a smile, they can pass different emotions around the circle such as anger, excitement, surprise, delight, sadness, and happiness. The teacher may have to pre-teach some of the emotions beforehand. The objective is to be aware of the movement they use on their face and body to express different emotions.

Game: Body Shapes
Level: Beginners+
Other benefits: This activity focus on shapes but it also helps with communication and teamwork skills.
Minimum number of participants: 4
Resources needed: Clear space and pictures of various shapes.
Instructions: Divide the students into groups of 4. The teacher calls out a shape such as square. Each group must try to work together to make that shape with their body. Everyone in the group must have some part of their body in the shape. The teacher gives them 30 seconds to complete. When the 30 seconds have elapsed, the groups stop. The teacher decides which group has made the best shape with their bodies and awards them a point. The group at the end with the most points is the winner.
Shape suggestions:

Basic shapes
- *Circle*
- *Square*
- *Rectangle*
- *Triangle*
- *Oval*

Advanced shapes
- *Trapezoid*
- *Parallelogram*
- *Pentagon*
- *Hexagon*
- *Octagon*
- *Diamond*
- *Star*
- *Heart*
- *Arrow*
- *Crescent*
- *Cube*

Improvisation

Improvisation is an effective way for ESL students to develop language skills that they can use outside of the classroom. Improvisation develops skills such as confidence and empathy. The following activities give students an outlet to express a range of emotions. A variety of tenses, vocabulary, question forms, idioms and proverbs are the focus of this section.

Game: Forwards/Backwards
Level: Elementary+
Other benefits: The main language is to practice target language and the present tense.
Minimum number of participants: 2
Resources needed: Clear space and copies of simple dialogues; see below for examples. Any of the dialogues from the teaching language books can be used.
Instructions: Divide the group into pairs and give each pair a copy of a simple dialogue. Give each pair time to practice their dialogues. When they have memorised the dialogues, get them to perform them in front of the class. Get the group to repeat it in slow motion, fast forwards, hopping on one leg, replacing the words with numbers or the alphabet, backwards, or jumping up and down.

Dialogue 1: Introductions
Adam: Good morning. What's your name? Where are you from?
Anna: My name is Anna. I'm from America.
Adam: My name is Adam and I'm from Alaska.
Anna: Pleased to meet you. *(They shake hands.)*
Anna: Goodbye. *(Waves and walks off.)*
Adam: See you soon.

Dialogue 2: Giving directions
Betty: Hello, you look lost. Can I help you?
Brian: Yes, please. I'm looking for the football stadium. Do you know where it is?
Betty: Of course. Go straight *(points straight),* turn left and it is next to the big shopping centre.
Brian: Thank you very much.
Betty: You are welcome.
Brain: Goodbye. *(They wave goodbye.)*

Dialogue 3: Greetings
Carl: Hello, how are you?
Cathy: Not so good.
Carl: What's the matter?
Cathy: I've a headache.
Carl: I hope you feel better soon.
Cathy: Thank you.

Extension: If the students are comfortable, get them to continue the dialogue until it comes to a natural conclusion. This is a good introduction to improvised work.

Game: TV Channels
Level: Elementary+
Other benefits: The focus is to listen and be observant as well as to react quickly.
Minimum number of participants: 4
Resources needed: Clear space.
Instructions: A volunteer sits in the centre of the circle. The rest of the students are the TV channels. The student in the centre of the circle is watching the television. He/she is channel surfing. When they point to someone in the circle, they have turned on the channel. The person must speak; they can be a news channel, weather, sports, documentary comedy, drama, or a soap opera.
The channel surfer stays on the channel for about 30 seconds and then moves on. They can always come back to the same channel. Everyone should have a chance at being a TV station.

Game: News Programme
Level: Pre-Intermediate+
Other benefits: This improvisation promotes focus and listening skills. It also helps with vocabulary and a variety of grammar tenses.
Minimum number of participants: 2
Resources needend: Clear space, two chairs and recording equipment (optional).
Instructions: This is an extension of the previous activity, TV Channels. Get the students into pairs and then tell them are going to be two anchors of a news programme. They must carry on from one another.
Example:
Anchor 1: Welcome to the 9-o clock news.
Anchor 2: Our big story tonight is there has been a big earthquake in Japan.
Anchor 1: Over 10,000 people have died. Other stories tonight include a lion escaped from the zoo.
Anchor 2: But he was captured after two hours and no one was harmed. They can keep taking turns. The teacher can give them a few minutes to come up with their news stories.
Extension: Divide the class into groups of six. Tell each group that they are going to deliver a news programme. They must have at least three different news stories. One story must be very serious and one must be a light news story and one must be the weather. Give them some time to determine who is going to be the anchor; one must be the weather forecaster. Then they can be people at the scene of the news report such as journalists, witnesses, victims, etc. Give them at least 20 minutes to prepare and deliver it to the other groups in the class. You can always record it and play it back.

Game: Dramatize a Nursery Rhyme
Level: Elementary+
Other benefits: The main aim of this game is practice the present and past tenses.
Minimum number of participants: 4
Resources needed: Clear space and a nursery rhyme for each group. See the list below.
Instructions: Divide the class into groups of four or five students. Give each group a nursery rhyme. Give them five minutes to prepare and tell them after five minutes they must act out the nursery rhyme in front of their classmates. Explain to them that they can't just recite the nursery rhyme. They must put it into their own words. If they can do this comfortably, give them ten minutes to come up with an alternative ending and have them perform their alternative nursery rhymes in front of the other groups.

The following nursery rhymes can be used:

Twinkle, Twinkle, Little Star
Twinkle, twinkle, little star,
How I wonder what you are.
Up above the world so high,
Like a diamond in the sky.
Twinkle, twinkle, little star,
How I wonder what you are!

Mary Had a Little Lamb
Mary had a little lamb,
Little lamb, little lamb,
Mary had a little lamb,
Whose fleece was white as snow.
And everywhere that Mary went,
Mary went, Mary went,
And everywhere that Mary went,
The lamb was sure to go.
It followed her to school one day
School one day, school one day,
It followed her to school one day,
Which was against the rules.
It made the children laugh and play,
Laugh and play, laugh and play,
It made the children laugh and play
To see a lamb at school.

The Itsy Bitsy Spider

The itsy bitsy spider crawled up the water spout.
Down came the rain and washed the spider out.
Out came the sun and dried up all the rain,
And the itsy bitsy spider went up the spout again.

Hickory Dickory Dock

Hickory Dickory Dock,
The mouse ran up the clock.
The clock struck one,
The mouse ran down!
Hickory Dickory Dock.

Little Bo Peep

Little Bo-peep has lost her sheep,
And doesn't know where to find them.
Leave them alone and they'll come home,
Wagging their tails behind them.
Little Bo-peep fell fast asleep,
And dreamt she heard them bleating;
But when she awoke, she found it a joke,
For they were still a-fleeting.
Then up she took her little crook,
Determined for to find them;
She found them indeed, but it made her heart bleed,
For they'd left all their tails behind them.

Jack and Jill

Jack and Jill went up the hill
To fetch a pail of water.
Jack fell down and broke his crown
And Jill came tumbling after.

Game: Fairy Tale Hot Seat
Level: Elementary+
Other benefits: The focus here is character development and question formation.
Minimum number of participants: 4
Resources needed: A clear space, a list of fairy-tale characters.
Instructions: Each student chooses the main character in a fairy tale (see list below for suggestions) and makes a role in the wall (see Drama Techniques section). After they build a character profile, they must walk around like their character. Are they angry or shy, happy or sad? They experiment with gesture and voice. To develop the character further, in small groups, they complete a hot seating exercise (see Drama Techniques section). Each student gets a chance to be on the Hot Seat and they interview each other's characters. They could write a monologue and perform it the next time they come to class.
Suggested characters:

- *Cinderella*
- *The Troll (from Three Billy Goats' Gruff)*
- *Snow White*
- *The Wicked Queen*
- *The Bad Fairy (from Sleeping Beauty)*
- *Gingerbread Man*
- *The Wicked Wolf*
- *Little Bo Peep*
- *Pinocchio*
- *Jack (from Jack and Jill)*
- *Jill*
- *The Beast (from Beauty and the Beast)*
- *Little Miss Muffet*
- *One of the Three Little Pigs*
- *Prince Charming*
- *Jack (from Jack and the Beanstalk)*
- *Ugly Duckling*
- *Fairy Godmother*

Game: Flash Forward/Flash Backwards
Level: Elementary+
Other benefits: The focus of this exercise is to practice past and future tenses.
Minimum number of participants: 4
Resources needed: Clear space and a list of newspaper headlines.
Instructions: Divide the class into groups of four. Tell them to choose a headline from the list of suggestions below:
Suggestions:
- *Huge car pileup on the motorway.*
- *The dog is a hero.*
- *Workers on strike for the third time.*
- *Famous star comes to town.*
- *Terror alert in the capital.*
- *More exams for students.*
- *Woman held for murder.*
- *Building collapses.*
- *Earthquake death toll rises.*

After each group, has chosen their headline, give them up to fifteen minutes to come up with two scenes. The first scene is a flash backward. They must improvise what happened before the headline. The second scene is a flash forward of what happened after the headline. When the fifteen minutes is completed, each group performs their flash forward and flash backward for the rest of the class.

Game: Idioms in Action
Level: Pre-Intermediate+
Other benefits: This is a fun and effective way to introduce idioms to ESL students.
Minimum number of participants: 4
Resources needed: Clear space and a list of idioms.
Instructions: The teacher explains the definition of an idiom. An idiom is a commonly used expression whose meaning doesn't relate to the literal meaning of the words. Ask the students for examples of idioms in their own languages. Divide the class into groups of four. Give each group an idiom. Each group discusses their idiom. Do they know what it means? What do they think it means? Give each group some time to prepare a short scene that relates to their idiom. Each group performs their idiom to the rest of the class.
Suggested Idioms:

- *The best of both worlds*
- *Break a leg*
- *When pigs fly*
- *Once in a blue moon*
- *A piece of cake*
- *To feel under the weather*
- *To kill two birds with one stone*
- *To cut corners*
- *To hit the nail on the head*

Game: Proverbs
Level: Pre-Intermediate+
Other benefits: The main aim is to introduce proverbs to the class.
Minimum number of participants: 4
Resources needed: Clear space and a list of proverbs.
Instructions: The teacher explains the definition of a proverb (wisdom tales without a plot). Ask the students for examples of proverbs in their own languages. Divide the class into groups of four. Have students choose a familiar proverb and develop a story that can surround and carry that thought.
Give each group some time to prepare a short improvisation that represents their proverb. Each group performs their improvisation to the rest of the class.
Suggested proverbs:
- *Two wrongs don't make a right.*
- *The pen is mighty than the sword.*
- *When in Rome, do what the Romans do.*
- *Fortune favours the bold.*
- *Better late than never.*
- *There's no such thing as a free lunch.*
- *The early bird catches the worm.*
- *You can't always get what you want.*
- *Actions speak louder than words.*
- *Practice makes perfect.*

Storytelling Activities

Storytelling games are very important in any learning environment. They are particularly important when working with ESL students as they encourage them to use their imaginations. The games also help to instil confidence in students and develop both their receptive and expressive skills. The following activities are a fun and enjoyable way of developing storytelling techniques. A variety of tenses, comparatives, adjectives, nouns, verbs, conjunctions, vocabulary, question formation and different parts of speech are the main language aspects that are practiced in this section.

Game: Story Stones
Level: Elementary+
Other benefits: This activity practices sequencing and develops the students' imagination.
Minimum number of participants: 2
Resources needed: Story stones or the materials to make the stones.
Instructions: Story stones are smooth, flat stones. Each stone has a picture of a character, animal or object on it. The story stone can be created in many ways. The students can paint a picture on it, or they can draw on the stone with a permanent marker. Alternatively, they can use cut-outs or fabric scraps to make their story stones. All the stones are put in a tray. One student chooses a stone and they start a story. Each student picks a stone and uses it to add to the story.

Game: Movement Story: The Hare and Tortoise
Level: Elementary+
Other benefits: This is an excellent listening game but it also practises the past tense, comparatives and adjectives.
Minimum number of participants: 1
Resources needed: Clear space and a copy of the story below.
Instructions: Ask the students if they know the story of the tortoise and the hare. Tell them you are going to tell them the story but instead of just sitting and listening, they are going to participate in the story. Tell them that they are going to listen for the following words and they must do the action associated with that word when they hear it in the story. The teacher should explain any words that the students might not understand, such as "boastful," which is telling everyone how good you are at something. The teacher should go through the different words and their movement. If there are too many words for the age group, the teacher can omit some of them. Once the teacher has gone through the words and the actions, she then shouts out words randomly to see if everyone knows the action. The students find their own space in the room so they can move freely and then the story can begin.
Boast/boastful/boasting—stand up straight and puff out chest.
Woods—students make themselves into trees.
Animals—each student chooses a different animal found in the woods and moves like that animal.
Hare—make bunny ears with your hands.
Fast—students move as fast as they can.
Run—run on the spot.
Tortoise—students bend over as if they have something heavy on their back.

Slow—students move in slow motion around the room.

Narrator: Once upon a time there was a very **boastful hare** that lived in the **woods** with lots of other **animals**. He was always **boasting** about how **fast** he could **run**. He **boasted,** "I'm the **fastest** animal in the woods. No one can **run** as **fast** as me." The other **animals** were tired of listening to him. One day, the **tortoise** said to the **hare,** "Hare, you are so **boastful.** I challenge you to a race." **Hare** laughed and said, "**Tortoise,** you will never beat me. You are too **slow** and steady." They decided whoever got to the other side of the **woods** the **fastest** was the winner. All the other **animals** in the **woods** came to watch the race. The **hare ran** as **fast** as he could through the **woods**. After a while, he thought to himself, "I'm so **fast** that **slow** tortoise will never beat me. I think I will take a quick nap." Soon he fell asleep. The **tortoise** walked **slowly** through the **woods.** He passed the sleeping **hare**. The **animals** watched the **tortoise** near the finishing line. The **animals** cheered loudly. The **hare** woke up and **ran** as **fast** as he could through the **woods** to the finishing line but it was too late. The **slow tortoise** had won the race. All the **animals** in the **woods** congratulated the **tortoise.** The **hare** had to remind himself that he shouldn't **boast** about his **fast** pace because **slow** and steady won the race.

Closure: Do you think the hare was boastful after the race? Why not? What lesson did we learn from the story? Now I want you to be your chosen animal again. All the animals stand in a straight line. The teacher explains that they are going to have a race but they must move in slow motion.

Game: Original Fables
Level: Elementary+
Other benefits: This is an enjoyable game that focuses on the past simple tense. It will teach the students about fables and morals.
Minimum number of participants: 2
Resources needed: Clear space, a copy of a fable. You can use the movement story above.
Instructions: The class listens to the story; ask them the moral of the fable. The class is divided into groups and they must devise their own fable. Explain to the class that a fable is a short story. Fables typically involve animals with human-like qualities. Usually in a fable, the time and the place are unspecified. Often fables illustrate how smaller and weaker characters use their intelligence to defeat the bigger and more powerful characters. There is always a hero, a villain, a character with a weakness and most importantly a moral. A moral is a lifelong lesson.

The most common characters found in fables are:
Rabbit
Fox
Crow
Bear
Rooster
Duck
Pig
Eagle
Hen
Wolf
Monkey
Donkey
Mouse
Rat
Cow
Goose
Lion
Boy
Girl

There are always good characters and evil characters in fables.
Examples of good characters:
Mouse
Kitten
Bunny
Cow

Examples of evil characters:
Snake
Lion
Rat
Bear

Using the template, get each group to devise their own fable.
Title:
Characters:
Hero:
Villain:
Character with a weakness:
Setting:
Problem:
Solution:
Trickery:
Moral:
Each group can tell or perform their fable to the rest of the class.

Game: A Shell's Life Story
Level: Beginners+
Other benefits: This game practices adjectives and the past tense.
Minimum number of participants: 3
Resources needed: A collection of different types of shells. The shells can be replaced by other objects, such as books, shoes, stones, chairs.
Instructions: Everyone sits in a circle. Different types of shells are passed around the circle. The students must come up with an adjective such as rough, smooth, hard, soft, big, or small to describe each shell. Divide the class into groups of three or four students in a group. Each group chooses a shell. They must come up with a life story about the shell. How did the shell land on the beach? How old is the shell? Does the shell have any family? What happened on its journey to the classroom? Give the students some time to come up with their story. Tell them that they can be as imaginative as they wish. Each group must tell the rest of the class their shell's life story.

Game: Four Ws: Who, What, Where, When.
Level: Pre-Intermediate+
Other benefits: This game focuses on vocabulary development and gives students an opportunity to practice different type of tenses.
Minimum number of participants: 4
Resources needed: Four categories of cards with who, what, where, and when on them.
Instructions: Divide the class into groups of four. Each member of the group chooses a card from a different category. Each group should end up with a who, what, where and when card. They must make up a story based on their cards. When each group has developed their story, either tell or act it out for the rest of the class.

Some ideas for the various categories:

Who:
- *An Alien*
- *An Astronaut*
- *A Lion*
- *A Prisoner*
- *The Devil*
- *A Witch*
- *A Ballerina*
- *A Strong-woman*
- *A Dinosaur*
- *A Policeman*

Where:
- *Jungle*
- *Under the sea*
- *Moon*
- *Mars*
- *Arctic*
- *Mount Everest*
- *Hell*
- *Desert*
- *Prison*
- *Farm*

What:
- *Can't stop running*
- *Lost the use of voice*
- *Woke up and lost a leg*
- *Caused a plane crash*
- *Can only say yes or no*

- *Under a spell*
- *In a very strange place*
- *Lost a very expensive watch*
- *Won the lottery*
- *Falls into a pig sty*

When:
- *Past*
- *Present*
- *Future*

Game: Random Words
Level: Elementary+
Other benefits: Noun, verbs, adjectives and conjunctions are all practised in this game.
Minimum number of participants: 1
Resources needed: A clear space, lists of nouns, verbs, adjectives and conjunctions.
Instructions: Each student chooses four words: a noun, verb, adjective, and conjunction. The story can be about anything but it must contain each of the four words. The story should have a beginning, middle and an end; each student gets an opportunity to share the story with the rest of the group.

Examples of simple words:

Nouns:
- *Person*
- *Year*
- *Thing*
- *World*
- *Life*
- *Place*
- *Work*
- *Problem*
- *Week*

Adjectives:
- *Annoyed*
- *Bad*
- *Beautiful*
- *Clever*

- *Dull*
- *Famous*
- *Lazy*
- *Rich*
- *Shy*
- *Tired*

Verbs:

- *Be*
- *Have*
- *Do*
- *Say*
- *Get*
- *Make*
- *Go*
- *Know*
- *Take*
- *See*

Conjunctions:

- *And*
- *That*
- *But*
- *So*
- *As*
- *If*
- *When*
- *Then*
- *Because*
- *After*

Game: Bring Me to Life
Level: Elementary+
Other benefits: This game allows the students to form and ask questions.
Minimum number of participants: 4
Resources needed: Images and a list of questions for each group.
Instructions: The students are divided into groups and are given an image and a list of questions. They must use their bodies to make an image of the object. The other groups ask questions such as:

- *What's your name?*
- *What are you like?*
- *What's your favourite colour?*
- *What's your favourite food?*
- *Where did you go on your holidays?*

Extension: Bring the object to life. The groups give a biographical background to their objects. They can have a few moments to write this down; they then present the biographical background to the rest of the groups.

Game: Still Image Dictation
Level: Elementary+
Other benefits: Simple present and present continuous tenses are used in this game.
Minimum number of participants: 4
Resources needed: A clear space.
Instructions: Give each group a different scenario and give them a few minutes to come up with a still image to depict the scene. When each group is ready, get them to freeze in their still image at the front of the class. When each group is ready get them to freeze in their still image at the front of the class. The other groups describe the scene.

Examples of scenarios:
You lost your mobile phone
Car crash
Lion escapes from the circus
Bank robbery

Extension: For more advanced students, the still images come to life and they start to improvise.

Game: Story Sentence
Level: Pre-Intermediate+
Other benefits: Parts of speech are focused on in this game.
Minimum number of participants: 6
Resources needed: A clear space.
Instructions: Everyone sits in a circle. Each person adds one word to the story. The word can't be a preposition, an adjective or a pronoun. You can put rules into the game.

Game: First-liners/Last-Liners
Level: Pre-Intermediate+
Other benefits: This is an excellent activity to develop story sequencing.
Minimum number of participants: 4
Resources needed: Clear space.
Instructions: Divide the class into groups of three or four. Give each group a line and the students must come up with a story that starts with that line.
Examples:
- *It was a dark and stormy night.*
- *"Wake up! Wake up!" she screamed.*
- *"Oh, look what has happened," she sighed. "I told you not to eat it."*
- *"I wouldn't go into that room if I were you," she said.*

An extension of this activity is that each group gets a sentence that the story must finish with:
- *And then he ate the goldfish.*
- *"Quick, run!"*
- *"I was only joking," he said.*
- *She couldn't believe how much money she owed.*

It is important to give the children 10 or 15 minutes to come up with their stories. Each group then must narrate its story, with every student contributing.

Puppet Activities

Puppets are an excellent resource to encourage learners' creativity, and imagination and to help the student practice their language skills in an ESL setting. The puppets enable the learners to communicate more freely in their target language. The learners become less concerned about making mistakes because it is the puppet that is speaking and not them. The use of puppets in the ESL classroom is an excellent way to encourage the more reserved language learner.

Using puppets in a language classroom need not be an expensive endeavour.

Hand puppets can be bought cheaply on eBay; an alternative is to buy old stuffed toys from charity shops and take out the stuffing. This is a cheap and effective way of building up a collection of puppets.

- *Sock puppets*
- *Finger puppets*
- *Paper plate puppets*
- *Newspaper puppets*
- *Brown paper bag puppets*

In addition, the learners can have lots of fun making their own puppets.

Game: Puppets at the Party
Level: Pre-Intermediate+
Other benefits: Greetings/introductions are practiced in this activity.
Minimum number of participants: 4
Resources needed: Clear Space and variety of different puppets.
Instructions: Each student chooses a puppet. Each puppet is at a party and he meets and greets the other puppets at the party. Sit in a circle and each puppet takes a turn saying who he/she met at the party.

Game: Blind Storyteller
Level: Intermediate+
Other benefits: This is an excellent activity to stimulate the students' imagination and to practice fluency.
Minimum number of participants: 4
Resources needed: Clear space and a variety of puppets.
Instructions: Divide the class into groups of 4. One person chooses to be the storyteller. The rest of the group is behind the storyteller holding the puppets. The storyteller starts his story and the rest of group use the puppets behind him to act it out.

Game: Puppet Talk Show
Level: Pre-Intermediate+
Other benefits: This is a fun game to practice different question forms and it also helps develop improvisation skills.
Minimum number of participants: 8
Resources needed: Clear space and a variety of puppets.
Instructions: This talk show is all about puppets! Have three people come up and sit at the front. Also, have a talk show "host" who leads the show. Have the puppets introduce themselves (they could be regular puppets or they could be famous people. For example, Elvis, Miley Cyrus, Cinderella, Justin Bieber). The "audience" members get to put up their hands and ask the puppets questions. You can use markers or sticks as microphones for the puppets to speak into. The host can encourage interaction between puppet guests as well as audience members.

Game: Puppet Music Videos
Level: Elementary+
Other benefits: This is a fun and easy game to revise specific vocabulary.
Minimum number of participants: 4
Resources needed: Clear space, a variety of puppets and access to a variety of English music.
Instructions: Have the group divide into small groups. Have them pick out their own music and make up a music video to show the group. The song must be in English.

Game: What If?
Level: Pre-Intermediate+
Other benefits: The focus of this game is to stimulate the students' imagination. Teamwork and problem solving skills are developed.
Minimum number of participants: 3
Resources needed: Clear space and a variety of puppets.
Instructions: Three or four students are chosen. Each chooses a puppet and stands at the front of the group. The audience or teacher asks a "what if?" question, for example, what if you missed the bus to work? The group would then have to act out that scenario, coming up with a solution. Once they were finished, you could have other volunteers come up and act out alternate endings.

Game: Puppet Show
Level: Elementary +
Other benefits: Co-operation and improvisation skills are practiced in this game.
Minimum number of participants: 4
Resources needed: Clear space and a variety of puppets.
Instructions: Have the class break into smaller groups and come up with their own puppet show ideas. Each group performs their puppet show to the rest of the class.

Game: Future Robot
Level: Pre-Intermediate+
Other benefits: This game can be used to practise future tenses.
Minimum number of participants: 4
Resources needed: Clear space and a variety of puppets.
Instructions: Teacher asks the class how they imagine life in 2,000 years and suggests to them that robots nowadays provide many services that humans provided years ago. Tell the students to create robot puppets of the future using their imagination. They must use different recycled materials to better preserve the earth. The robot should be designed to do a specific job in the future that the student chooses.

Game: Emotional Puppets
Level: Elementary+
Other benefits: Emotions and feelings are practised in this activity.
Minimum number of participants: 4
Resources needed: Clear space and a variety of puppets.
Instructions: Give each student an emotion and then get them to choose a puppet that best represents that emotion. Go back to the party and talk to all the other puppets. After enough time, get them to sit down in a circle again and go through the circle one by one. Ask the group what each puppet's emotion was. Ask them how they knew. How did the puppet make it obvious?

Game: Me as a Puppet
Level: Elementary+
Other benefits: This game practises personal descriptions and comparatives.
Minimum number of participants: 4
Resources needed: Clear space and puppet-making materials.
Instructions: Give each person in the group various puppet making supplies and have them make a puppet that reflects them. I suggest sticking to one kind of puppet, such as a paper plate stick puppet. The puppets do not have to look exactly like the person. Instead they could have some of the person's attributes such as being shy, loud, having freckles or glasses. The rest of the puppet could be imagined, or what the person would like to look like if he had the choice. After making the puppets, you might sit in a circle and introduce the puppets. An interesting script might be to say one thing or two things about your puppet that is the same as you and one thing that is different.

Part Two: Plays

Little Bunny Foo Foo

Characters: Little Bunny Foo Foo, three storytellers, nine mice and the Blue Fairy

Storyteller 1: Once upon a time, there was a rabbit call Little Bunny Foo Foo.

Storyteller 2: He liked nothing more than hopping through the forest,

Storyteller 3: and scooping up the field mice and bopping them on the head.

(Little Bunny Foo Foo jumps around the stage picking up the field-mice and bopping them on the head.)

Mouse 1: Ouch! That hurts!

Mouse 2: Stop it.

Mouse 3: We will tell the Blue Fairy.

Storyteller 1: Down came the Blue Fairy, and she said:

Blue Fairy: Little Bunny Foo Foo, I don't want to see you scooping up the field mice and bopping them on the head. Now I'll give you three chances, and if you keep it up, I'll turn you into a goon.

(Little Bunny Foo Foo hangs his head in shame and the Blue Fairy leaves. Little Bunny Foo Foo hops around the stage and looks around and when he thinks the Blue Fairy isn't looking, he starts bopping the field-mice on the head.)

Storyteller 2: Little Bunny Foo Foo kept hopping through the forest.

Storyteller 3: He kept scooping up the field-mice and bopping them on the head.

Mouse 4: Ouch! That hurts.

Mouse 5: Stop it.

Mouse 6: We will tell the Blue Fairy.

Storyteller 1: Down came the Blue Fairy, and she said:

Blue Fairy: Little Bunny Foo Foo, I don't want to see you scooping up the field-mice and bopping them on the head. Now I'll give you two more chances, and if you do that again, I'll turn you into a goon. *(Little Bunny Foo Foo hangs his head in shame and the Blue Fairy leaves. Little Bunny Foo Foo hops around the stage and looks around, and when he thinks the Blue Fairy isn't looking, he starts bopping the field-mice on the head.)*

Storyteller 2: Little Bunny Foo Foo kept hopping through the forest.

Storyteller 3: He kept scooping up the field-mice and bopping them on the head.

Mouse 7: Ouch! That hurts!

Mouse 8: Stop it.

Mouse 9: We will tell the Blue Fairy.

Storyteller 1: Down came the Blue Fairy, and she said:

Blue Fairy: Little Bunny Foo Foo, I don't want to see you scooping up the field-mice and bopping them on the head. Now I'll give you one more chance, and if you do that again, I'll turn you into a goon. (*Little Bunny Foo Foo hangs his head in shame and the Blue Fairy leaves. Little Bunny Foo Foo hops around the stage and looks around and when he thinks the Blue Fairy isn't looking he starts bopping the field-mice on the head.*)

Storyteller 2: Little Bunny Foo Foo kept hopping through the forest.

Storyteller 3: He kept scooping up the field-mice and bopping them on the head.

Storyteller 1: Down came the Blue Fairy, and she said:

Blue Fairy: Little Bunny Foo Foo, I don't want to see you scooping up the field-mice and bopping them on the head. You disobeyed me three times, so now I'm going to turn you into a goon! (*Blue Fairy waves her magic wand and turns Little Bunny Foo Foo into a goon. All the mice laugh.*)

Storytellers: The lesson of this story is, Hare today, Goon tomorrow!

The Three Little Pigs

Character: First Little Pig, Second Little Pig, Third Little Pig, Mother, Man with Straw, Man with Sticks, Man with Bricks, Big Bad Wolf, and the Three Storytellers

Storyteller 1: Once upon a time, there lived three little pigs.

Storyteller 2: They lived at home with their mother.

Storyteller 3: One day, their mother said:

Mother: You are old enough to go out into the world and make it on your own.

Storyteller 1: She gave them some food and said goodbye. *(She gives them some food and they all hug her.)*

Mother: Bye, bye. *(She waves goodbye.)*

Little Pigs: Bye, Mother. *(They wave at their mother.)*

First Little Pig: It's so exciting to be out in the world by ourselves. *(A man with straw passes by.)*

First Little Pig: Please, Sir, may I have some straw so I can build a house of my very own?

Man, with Straw: Certainly, here you go. *(Man, gives the First Little Pig straw and he starts to build his house.)*

Storyteller 2: The other two pigs said goodbye and continued their way. *(They all hug each other and they wave goodbye.)*

Second Little Pig: It's so exciting be out in the world by ourselves. *(A man with sticks passes by.)*

Second Little Pig: Please, sir, may I have some sticks so I can build a house of my very own?

Man, with Sticks: Certainly, here you go. *(Man, gives the Second Little Pig sticks and he starts to build his house.)*

Storyteller 3: The Third Little Pig said goodbye and continued his way. *(He hugs his brother and goes on his way.)*

Third Little Pig: It's so exciting be out in the world by myself. *(A man with bricks passes by.)*

Third Little Pig: Please, sir, may I have some bricks so I can build a house of my very own?

Man, with Bricks: Certainly, here you go. (*Man, gives the Third Little Pig bricks and he starts to build his house.*)

Storyteller 1: The Third Little Pig made his house of bricks.

Story teller 2: One day a big, bad wolf came knocking at the first little pig's house.

Big Bad Wolf: *(knocks)* Little pig, little pig, let me come in!

First Little Pig: Not by the hair of my chinny-chin-chin.

Big Bad Wolf: Then I will huff and I will puff and I will blow your house down.

Storyteller 3: So, he huffed and he puffed and he blew the house in. (*The First Little Pig ran to his brother's house made of sticks.*)

First Little Pig: Help, help, the wolf is after me!

Second Little Pig: Come in and sit down; you will be safe here. (*He gives him a cup of tea.*)

Storyteller 1: One day a big, bad wolf came knocking on the Second Little Pig's house.

Big Bad Wolf: *(knocks)* Little pig, little pig, let me come in.

Second Little Pig: Not by the hair of my chinny-chin-chin.

Big Bad Wolf: Then I will huff and I will puff and I will blow your house in.

Storyteller 2: So, he huffed and he puffed and he blew the house in. (*The First and the Second Little Pigs run to their brother's house made of bricks.*)

First Little Pig/Second Little Pig: Help, help, the wolf is after us!

Third Little Pig: Come in and sit down; you will be safe here. (*He gives them cups of tea.*)

Storyteller 3: A few days later, the wolf came knocking on the Third Little Pig's door.

Big Bad Wolf: *(knocks)* Little pig, little pig, let me come in.

First Little Pig: Not by the hair of the chinny-chin-chin.

Big Bad Wolf: Then I will huff and I will puff and I will blow your house in.

Storyteller 1: So, he huffed and he puffed and huffed and he puffed and he huffed and he puffed but he couldn't blow the house in.

Storyteller 2: So, he decided to climb up on the roof. (The wolf mimes climbing up on the roof.)

First Little Pig: Did you hear that?

Second Little Pig: What?

Third Little Pig: Sssssssssh, It's the wolf on the roof. I've an idea put some water to boil on the fire. *(They mime putting a pot of boiling water on the fire.)*

Big Bad Wolf: Little pigs, I am coming to get you. Ohhh!

(Big Bad Wolf falls into the boiling water and runs out of the house screaming in pain. Three Little Pigs are laughing.)

Pigs: Ha! Ha!

Storyteller 3: And the Three Little Pigs lived happily ever after

The Enormous Turnip

Characters: Three storytellers, old man, old woman, boy, girl, dog, cat and mouse.

(Stage Directions: storytellers on stage left and the old man in the centre. All the other characters are in a line off-stage or they can be on stage, with each character miming doing their own thing.)

Storyteller 1: Once upon a time there lived a little old man.

Storyteller 2: One day he planted a turnip seed in his garden. (*Old man plants his seed.*)

Old Man: This turnip is going to be very big and very sweet. (*Looks at the audience.*)

Storyteller 3: The turnip grew and grew.

Old Man: I think it is time to dig up the turnip. *(Old man mimes trying to pull it up.)*

Storyteller 1: He pulled and pulled but he couldn't pull up the turnip.

Old Man: I know, I will ask my wife to help me. Wife! Wife! Please help me to pull up the turnip.

(Wife holds on to him at the waist and they try pulling up the turnip.)

Storyteller 2: His wife came and helped him.

Storyteller 3: They pulled and pulled but they couldn't pull up the turnip.

Wife: I know, I will ask the boy to help us. Boy! Boy! Please help us to pull up the turnip. (*She calls for the boy and the boy comes to help them.*)

Storyteller 1: The boy came and helped them. (*The boy holds on to her at the waist.*)

Storyteller 2: They pulled and pulled but they couldn't pull up the turnip.

Boy: I know. I will ask the girl to help us. Girl! Girl! Please help us to pull up the turnip. (*He calls for the girl and the girl comes to help them.*)

Storyteller 3: The girl came and helped them. (*The girl holds on to him at the waist.*)

Storyteller 1: They pulled and pulled but they couldn't pull up the turnip.

Girl: I know, I will ask the dog to help us. Dog! Dog! Please help us to pull up the turnip. (*She calls for the dog and the dog comes to help her.*)

Storyteller 2: The dog came and helped them. (*The dog holds on to her at the waist.*)

Storyteller 3: They pulled and pulled but they couldn't pull up the turnip.

Dog: I know, I will ask the cat to help us. Cat! Cat! Please help us to pull up the turnip. (*He calls for the cat and the cat comes to help them. The cat holds on to him at the waist.*)

Storyteller 1: The cat came and helped them.

Storyteller 2: They pulled and pulled but they couldn't pull up the turnip.

Cat: I know, I will ask the mouse to help us. Mouse! Mouse! Please help us to pull up the turnip. (*She calls for the mouse and the mouse comes to help them.*)

Storyteller 3: The mouse came and helped them. (*The mouse holds onto her at the waist.*)

Storyteller 1: They pulled and pulled and then suddenly they pulled up the turnip. (*They all fall over.*)

Storyteller 2: Everyone was very happy and they all thanked the mouse. (*Everyone shakes hands with the mouse.*)

Storyteller 3: Everyone had turnip soup for dinner. (*The wife mimes giving each one of them a bowl of soup and they mime drinking it.*)

King Midas

Characters: Three Narrators, King Midas, Dionysus, servant, Princess and Rover the dog

Narrator 1: In ancient Greece, there lived a King called Midas. King Midas loved money more than anything else in the world.

Narrator 2: He loved to count his gold every day. *(The king is sitting on the centre stage counting his bars of gold.)*

King Midas: 4,936, 4937, 4938, I love gold more than anything. It makes me so happy.

(Enter Dionysus.)

Dionysus: I want to thank you, Midas, for letting me stay with you. You have been very kind.

King Midas: I'm glad you enjoyed your stay, Dionysus. You know you are always welcome here.

Dionysus: Midas: I wish to show you my appreciation by granting you a wish.

Narrator 3: The king was delighted and he thought carefully what he could wish for.

King Midas: I wonder what I could possibly wish for? *(He thinks carefully for a while.)* I know. Dionysus, Dionysus! I know what I want. I want everything that I touch to turn to gold.

Dionysus: *(bows)* Your wish is my command, Your Majesty. From now on. everything you touch will turn to gold. Goodbye. *(King Midas goes to shake his hand but Dionysus avoids him and runs off.)*

King Midas: *(waves)* Goodbye Dionysus. Could it be true that everything I touch will turn to gold?

(He moves around the room and touches the chair. The chair turns to gold and becomes heavy and he struggles to carry it. He rubs his hands with glee and then touches a book and then the table and everything turns to gold.)

King Midas: *(does a little dance)* I'm going to be even richer than I was before. All this work is making me hungry. *(He tries to ring the bell for tea but that turns to gold and doesn't ring.)*

King Midas: Never mind. Servant! Servant!

(Servant enters.)

Servant: *(bows)* You called, Your Majesty.

King Midas: I'm hungry; bring me my tea.

Servant: Yes, Your Majesty. (He walks backwards while bowing.)

Narrator 1: The servant brought King Midas his tea.

(Enter servant with the food but everything turns to gold when the king touches it. He tries eating it with just his mouth but that doesn't work and his mouth hurts trying to eat the food.)

King Midas: Oh, dear, I'm so hungry. Servant, bring me my tennis racket and ball. *(Servant brings him the tennis racket and ball and everything turns to gold. Rover the dog comes in and tries to get the ball and give it to the king but it is too heavy.)*

Rover: Woof! Woof!

King Midas: Good boy, Rover. (He pats him and he turns to gold.)

King Midas: Poor Rover, but you will look good as a statue in the hall.

(the princess enters.)

Princess: *(calling for Rover)* Rover? Rover? Daddy, have you seen Rover. Oh, my, what a beautiful statue of Rover.

King Midas: You can have it if you like.

Princess: Oh, thank you, Daddy. *(She goes to hug him.)*

King Midas: Please don't touch… *(King Midas tries to avoid her but it is too late and she turns to gold.)*

King Midas: Oh, no! what have I done? I have turned my only daughter into gold. *(He starts to cry.)* Dionysus, Dionysus, please come back. I have been so selfish. I'm so sorry.

(Dionysus appears.)

Dionysus: I think you have learned your lesson. I will take away your magic wish only if you promise not to love money so much.

(The princess and the dog start to move and they hug King Midas.)

Narrator 3: From that day on, Midas was never selfish or greedy again.

It is Better to Forget

Characters: Jane, Lisa, Jack, two police officers

(Lisa is sitting in a farm kitchen. Jane comes in and puts her gun on the table.)

Lisa: Is everything locked up for the night?

Jane: I think so.

Lisa: You should have done it much earlier. You always keep putting things off until the last minute.

Jane: *(sighs and puts her eyes up to heaven)* Oh, Lisa, just because I forgot to make my bed yesterday doesn't mean you need to keep going on about it. You are like a broken record.

Lisa: And you didn't get around to collecting the eggs for three whole days.

Jane: Alright, alright, I know: I forgot. I will get them now.

Lisa: Aren't you scared, going around the farm in the dark?

Jane: No, I have my gun. *(Picks the gun up and shows it to Lisa.)* It is lonely here in winter on our own and we need protection. Sometimes I wish we'd never inherited this place.

Lisa: Have some tea, you will feel better. *(Jane pours out a cup of tea and both sit on the table.)*

Jane: I know it is lonely, but it is lovely in the summer.

Lisa: *(starts making faces)* Oh Jane, you forgot to put the sugar in. (hears something) What's that?

Jane: There is someone at the door.

Jack: *(bursting in the door)* Don't speak! *(looks around and he picks up the gun)* Don't move or you are dead. Get me some food.

(Lisa is terrified but Jane is calmer.)

Jack: *(points the gun at Jane)* Get me some food quickly. Don't look for help or you will be sorry.

(Jane goes off to get him food. She makes a 'phone call quickly.)

Jane: You must be the prisoner that escaped this morning. I heard it on the news. You have come a long way. *(She gives him some tea and bread. He devours it.)* *(Jack eats greedily keeping the gun pointed at theme; there're is a loud knocking at the door.)*

Jack: If you open the door I'll shoot you.

(Jane walks to the door ignoring him. Lisa faints.) (Jack pulls the trigger and nothing happens. Jane opens the door and two police officers walk in.)

First police officer: There you are. *(They grab Jack.)* A most dangerous criminal wanted several crimes including murder. *(looks at Jane)* You were ever so brave to phone us.

Second police officer: Yes, you were indeed. You stay quiet. *(Looks at Jack who is struggling.)*

Lisa: Oh Jane, you were so brave, but he could have killed us with that gun.

Jane: Nonsense. The gun wasn't loaded. I took out the cartridges ready to clean it this morning. I just didn't get around to doing it and I forgot to put it back.

The Body

Characters: Two Narrators, Stomach, Brain, Eyes, Hands, Feet and Teeth

(All characters are on stage. They are miming working.)

Narrator 1: Once upon a time, a long time ago, the parts of the body did not work as well as they do now.

Stomach: *(clicks his fingers)* Brain, Brain, I'm hungry. Think of something I can eat. *(lying down centre stage.)*

Brain: Well, let me think about a healthy green salad. *(He hands stomach some salad.)*

Stomach: That's too planty. *(Stomach makes a face.)*

Brain: Well how about some delicious home-made soup?

Stomach: No, too sloppy!

Brain: *(sighs)* Some French fries?

Stomach: No, too greasy!

Brain: I have got a burger. *(Brain throws his eyes to heaven.)*

Stomach: No, too heavy and meaty. Come on, Brain, THINK, THINK, WILL YOU!

Brain: *(to audience)* Think, think. It's alright for him just to sit there and shout 'think.' It is getting a bit much – day in, day out, having to think what to feed him. *(turns to stomach.)* I know what should do the trick – how about a perfect pepperoni and pineapple pizza?

Stomach: That's it. That will do nicely. *(He shouts.)* Eyes! Eyes!–Come here! Go and check if the pizza is good enough to eat.

Eyes: Okay, Stomach. *(He goes off to look for the pizza.)*

Stomach: Feet, go with eyes and help to bring it back. Where are Hands? Come on what are you waiting for – help. I don't know: these parts of the body are getting lazy! Hurry up would you, I am STARVING!

Hands: Here you are, Stomach. *(gives Stomach the pizza.)*

Stomach: What is this? There is no pineapple on it. Take it back and get me what I want, now! Don't you have a lot brain? *(Throws the pizza at Hands, Feet and Eyes.)*

Feet: I don't know who he thinks he is.

Hands: What a cheek.

Brain: I'm sick of this. Let's get him a pizza with pineapple, feed him and then when he's asleep we'll call a meeting of the body parts.

All: Right Come on!

Hands: Here you are, Stomach. I hope you enjoy it. Come on, Teeth and Tongue – do your job so Stomach can get his food. *(Stomach eats the pizza and goes to sleep.)*

Narrator 2: So, Teeth and Tongue helped to chew and swallow the pizza. Stomach was so full afterwards that he fell asleep. The body parts all gathered around to discuss what they could do about the bossy Stomach.

Brain: Listen, everyone, I've called this meeting about Stomach. He is getting on my nerves! What do you think, Hands?

Hands: He's so lazy. We work hard all day and he does nothing but accept the food we give to him.

Feet: You are right! We work hard too. We walk miles every day, mostly getting food for him, yet he does no work.

Teeth: It's true. Just think of all the work I do chewing his food while he just sits there doing nothing.

Eyes: I've being playing "I Spy" with Stomach; all he ever spies is food and more food.

Brain: I have a plan: let's teach him a lesson. I think we should stop feeding Stomach. He is so lazy he doesn't deserve our help. Is everyone agreed?

All: Agreed.

Narrator 2: They continued with this plan for several days.

The Brain would not think of food.

The Feet would not walk to get food.

The Eyes would not look at food.

The Hands would not hold a knife or fork to carry food.

The Mouth wouldn't open to let food in and the Tongue and Throat would not swallow.

(The parts of the body were pleased with themselves but not for long. Soon each part began to feel weak and wobbly.)

Brain: 1+1=...1, 2+1=0 ...2, 4=1 + Oh, I am all confused. I can hardly think at all.

Feet: I can hardly walk.

Eyes: I can't focus properly.

Hands: I can't grip anything.

Teeth: I'm so sore, I am falling out!

All: What's happening to us?

Stomach: I know what is happening. I can't live without all your parts working for me but now perhaps you realise that you can't live without me either. We all need each other. I'm sorry if I was bossy. We must work together and then we will be all right. If you give me some fruit and vegetables, I will be as good as new.

Narrator 1: Well, they did just that and they were all as good as new. The body parts had learned their lesson and ever since they have worked together very well.

Drama Techniques

Ceremony: Groups devise special events to mark, commemorate or celebrate something of cultural/historical significance.

Choral Speak/Reading: All speaking at the same time, the same words, with one voice.

Conscience Alley: Two rows of students face each other. There is enough space between them for someone to walk down the middle. As one character walks, the rest of group plays the character's thoughts, and voices are lower in volume. A word or phrase is spoken as the character passes by individuals in the group. The two rows represent the character's conscience.

Creating a place: With only bodies and movement, and sometimes sound, students create a setting (like a stormy sea, a noisy playground, etc.).

Freeze Frame: A moment in a scene that is frozen.

Hot-seating: A specific seat is designated as the hot seat. One student volunteers to sit in the seat and assume a role. The rest of the students question the character to get to know him/her better, his/her point of view, background, views on the other characters and/or problems in the story.

Improvisation: A dramatic scene where dialogue, plot and setting are made up in the moment.

Interview: One student is given a response from another through questioning to reveal information, attitudes or motives.

Mime: Action and storytelling without words.

Monologue: A speech presented by one character. It uses the first person. It can reveal inner thoughts, emotions, a story, secrets or answers to questions.

Narration: This can be done in or out of the dramatic context. A way to provide a narrative link, atmosphere, initiate a drama, move the action on, create tension.

Narrative Pantomime: Student/teacher narrates a scene while the group mimes the action/story.

Reflection: Group discussion and share about what was seen, what was learned and what did we like.

Role on the Wall: Students are writing on a paper outline figure of character first impressions and information they learn about the character as they discover the character in the story or play. Students are seeing that the better we know someone, the better we understand them, and they are seeing a character transformed.

Still Image/Tableau: Frozen action, a picture, book illustration, or photograph.

Teacher in-Role: Teacher takes on a role as part of the story for students to interact with them inside the drama.

Thought Tracking: Usually used in conjunction with still image work where the teacher steps into the image to ask characters their innermost thoughts and feelings.

Writing in Role: Diaries, Letters, Journals, Messages. These are written in or out of role as a means of reflecting on experience. Students write as if they were the character writing a letter, in a personal journal, and so on. This is thinking in role, drawing information from what has already been collectively assembled. Students use their personal knowledge and imaginations to create the world of the character. This is a way to experience stream of consciousness writing.

Made in the USA
Las Vegas, NV
29 August 2023

76792452R00062